Newminster
Monks, Shepherds and Charters

The story of Northumberland's forgotten abbey

Bridget Gubbins
with original illustrations by
Victor Ambrus

Published by
Greater Morpeth Development Trust
2014

By the same author

The Mysteries of Morpeth's Workhouse, 2013
The Drovers are Coming to Morpeth Town, 2012
The Curious Yards and Alleyways of Morpeth, 2011
Published by Greater Morpeth Development Trust, with illustrations by Victor Ambrus

Power at Bay, 1997
Generating Pressure, 1991
Published by Earthright Publications

Published by:
Greater Morpeth Development Trust
Carlisle Park Lodge
Castle Square
Morpeth
Northumberland
NE61 1YD

Greater Morpeth
Development Trust
Regeneration of town & countryside
www.gmdt.net

First published 2014

British Library Cataloguing in Publication Data
A catalogue reference for this book is available from the British Library

ISBN 978-0-9568683-3-6

Original illustrations © Victor Ambrus
Front cover illustration by Victor Ambrus.
Church design guided and authorised by Glyn Coppack

Back cover photo from Newminster Cartulary, from the Castle Howard Archive.
Reproduced with kind permission of the Hon. Simon Howard.

Cover design by Azure Printing

Printed in Great Britain by Martins the Printers Ltd., Sea View Works, Spittal, Berwick upon Tweed, TD15 1RS

Newminster Abbey, 1971. View looking north-east
From the collection of the late Mr C R Warn in Northumberland Archives. NRO 6350-113

The abbey's remains are on private land and there is no public access

Contents

Acknowledgments. Pounds shillings and pence

Newminster: Monks, Shepherds and Charters

Acknowledgments

Greater Morpeth Development Trust, for their confidence and support
John Bibby, for reading and photo manipulation
Kim Bibby-Wilson, for reading and historical advice
Glyn Coppack, Cistercian architecture and history
David Cranston, salt works text
Rosie Cusson and Mary Harris, indomitable travel companions
Keith Elliott, research
John Griffiths, reading and support
Linsey Hunter, Latin translation and advice
David Jones, writing and reviewing text on the wool trade
Barry Mead, reading, guidance and archaeology advice
Morpeth Antiquarian Society, donation towards the cost of Latin translations
Teresa Saunders, Latin translation
George Thornton, for the germ of the idea

Many of the people who helped in all kinds of ways are acknowledged in the text.
Special thanks to all the below:

Dan Branda, the Candea family, Reuben Carrdus, Mary Creighton, Alan Davison, Cynthia Fair, Patrick Gubbins, Anne Harding, Garry Jenkins, Anna Louise Mason, Rod Mathieson, Colm O'Brien, Denis Peel, Neil and Leigh Purvis, Roz Ramshaw, Peter Ryder, Eric Waites, Kate Wilson and Sue Ward

All unacknowledged photos and drawings are by the author

Pounds, shillings and pence

Prior to 15 February 1971, money in this country was counted in pounds, shillings and pence. Most of the time when amounts of money appear in the text, they will use this form. There were twenty shillings to the pound and twelve pence to the shilling. Sometimes half pence may be mentioned. A farthing was a quarter of a penny. When Henry VIII's commissioners evaluated the properties of Newminster in 1536, the amount was calculated to the nearest farthing!

Marks were also sometimes used, and one mark was roughly two thirds of one pound.

Monks, shepherds and charters

"Please can you tell me if there is an English translation anywhere of the Newminster cartulary?"

I wrote this in an email to a well known archaeologist whose work had included translations of some of the abbey's charters. His reply?

"We don't think there is an English translation but we'd be happy to supply you with tea and biscuits if you want to attempt one!"

Newminster Abbey lies on the edge of Morpeth in Northumberland. Its remains are buried under heaps of vegetation and almost nothing can be seen from public viewpoints. I had decided I'd like to write its story. But how was I to do it?

The cartulary is the most detailed and important source of information about this hidden abbey. Two years of Latin at school in the 1950s was of very limited help. I knew this couldn't stop me and that I'd have to manage with the Latin version, together with any odd bits of translation I could find.

Chartularium Abbathiae de Novo Monasterio. The Cartulary of the Abbey of New Minster.

The cartulary is a collection of Newminster's charters which go back to 1138. Starting in 1876, Rev J T Fowler transferred the almost illegible pages of parchment into a readable version. He re-wrote the almost indecipherable medieval Latin in an accessible form. What a genius! I have nothing but admiration for him and I'm sure you will agree with me when you look at some photographs of the original in this book. He didn't translate it; he left that for the future.

With a copy of the 1876 book on my desk, I began the story which follows. Hidden in its pages are glimpses of places and people from long ago; the sentiments and religious fears of the noble families who granted land to the monks; and the great extent of the abbey's properties spreading out from its centre near Morpeth to the border hills and the sea.

The work of other great historians was essential too, principally Rev John Hodgson's histories of Northumberland and some of the Northumberland county histories written mainly at end of the 19th and early 20th century.

We can follow the story from the 1130s when Juliana Cospatric brought her dowry to her marriage with Ranulph de Merlay and to the arrival of Abbot Robert and the monks in 1138. We can trace the growth of the abbey with the people who looked after it in its golden years and its ultimate demise at the hands of Henry VIII in 1537. It is a great adventure.

What is more, for me, it was a literal adventure. It took me to Romania to learn about transhumance, the movement of the flocks, which was practised by the Newminster monks. And then my sister, my friend and I tracked the footsteps of the monks and the shepherds from the abbey to the Cheviots, guided by the charters.

I am hugely aware of my own ignorance in the many fields into which I've been obliged to venture. I've sought help from those with immense knowledge of Cistercian architecture, medieval Latin charters, Northumberland's history, the medieval wool trade, the dissolution of the monasteries by Henry VIII and much more. I offer up my efforts as a step on the way to further investigation by others. But, if you can accept that, come with me. Let's see what we can learn together about that almost forgotten abbey near Morpeth.

Old Bakehouse Yard, Morpeth, 2014   Bridget Gubbins

The signing and celebration of Juliana Cospatric's marriage contract between Henry I and her father, around the year 1133. The lands of her dowry would be passed to Newminster. Illustration by Victor Ambrus

1 Earliest origins

In the castle on the hill

Inside the wooden castle on the hummock of a hill in Morpeth, Northumberland, Ranulph and Juliana de Merlay are discussing their plans, while their children William, Roger and Osbert run in and out. It is autumn 1137 and soon the family will be welcoming a group of monks from Fountains who are arriving to establish a new abbey near the Wansbeck river.

Ranulph de Merlay is the son of William de Merlay, reckoned by historians to be the first lord of Morpeth after the Norman Conquest and who built the first motte and bailey castle on Ha' Hill in about 1080. Juliana is a daughter of the native Northumbrian noble family, the Cospatrics. The founding of the new monastery is an absorbing topic of conversation in the castle on the hill, in both French and English.

Morpeth hardly warrants the name *town* at this time. There are just a few lowly peasant houses on the north side of the river and a few more with perhaps a wooden church nearer the castle. The site which the family has chosen for the abbey is on cultivated land a quarter of a mile up river from the castle.

Ranulph, like the other Norman barons, moved freely around the aristocratic networks of the day, and in the course of doing so had visited Fountains in Yorkshire, where there was a newly founded Cistercian abbey. He'd been impressed by the piety of the monks, and decided he'd like to establish his own monastery on his land.

We may ask why he would do this. This was the great age of the spread of the new monastic orders across Europe; Benedictines, Premonstratensians, Gilbertines and Tironensians, and among the greatest and most influential of all, the Cistercians. There was huge prestige among the Norman nobility for establishing a monastery on their lands. Besides that, there was life after death to be considered. The monks would pray for the eternal souls of the founders and their families. There was a real fear of eternal damnation in the Christianity of those days. Warriors who'd survived violent battles, inflicting ghastly wounds on others and watching their own companions being mutilated must have had nightmarish fears about their own personal hell. The monks' prayers and piety would perhaps reduce their time in purgatory.

As well as prestige and the fear of hell, there was an economic incentive. The wealth of the nobility sprang essentially from the land and the goods produced by the labourers under their control. The monks were farmers and much of the land inherited by the likes of the de Merlays was undeveloped. The monks would turn it into productive agricultural land, with little effort on the part of the donors.

Three origin stories

The story of Newminster's earliest origins is recorded in three brief but fundamental sources. Versions of the story appear in Rev John Hodgson's *History of Morpeth* of 1832 and in later books such as Percy Hedley's *Northumberland Families* of 1968. The writers of many other local histories have used these as sources in their own right. Both Hodgson and Hedley quote earlier manuscripts and the evidence trail winds backwards into history, through several re-writings of earlier documents and manuscripts. For my own benefit and yours, I have tried to get as close as possible to the sources.

The first story originates in Prior John's history of Hexham, written some time shortly after 1154. The second is from a volume called *Memorials of Fountains Abbey,* the mother abbey of Newminster. The third is from Prior Richard's history of Hexham and tells us about the destruction of Newminster by the army of the Scots in the first year of its foundation. These stories were all written in Latin and it is fortunate that 19th century scholars have translated them for us. Let's look at them one at a time.

Prior John, in the 1138 section of his *History of the Church of Hexham*, tells us that Ranulph received the monks in Morpeth castle:

> In the same year a certain powerful man in Northumberland received on his property at the castle called Morpeth, on the nones of January (5 January) eight monks of Fountains, who built the monastery called Newminster: for whom, on the feast of Epiphany in this year, Geoffrey, bishop of Durham, consecrated as abbot the holy man Robert. Them the aforesaid man, namely, Ralph de Merlay, gladly favoured.[1]

That is all we find out about Newminster in Prior John's history.

The second story from the *Memorials of Fountains Abbey* tells us this:

> In the fifth year from the foundation of our mother, the monastery of Fountains, a certain nobleman, Ranulph de Merlay, came to visit our Fountains. Beholding the conversation of the brethren, the man is pricked to the heart, and, under the inspiration of God, assigns a certain place in his paternal estate in order to build a monastery for the redemption of his soul.
>
> The holy abbot receives the man's offering, and the buildings being set out therein after our manner, he builds the abbey, which he named the New Minster; and this was the first daughter of the holy church of Fountains, as yet the only one of her mother.
>
> In the sixth year of her foundation, in the first month, on the fifth day of the month, a convent is sent out from the house of Fountains to New Minster, with the abbot Robert, a holy and religious man, formerly a monk of Whitby, who allied himself with them when they went out from the York house. Of this man we have heard many things worthy of being related, to which a special treatise shall be devoted.
>
> For he was modest in bearing, gentle in social life, merciful in judgement, singular in holy conversation. For many years he both presided over and was profitable to the brethren as a holy father and excellent pastor, and he completed a holy conversation by a holier end. Blessed Godric, as we read in his life, saw one night, while praying, the soul of this holy man, released from the flesh, carried into heaven by the hands of angels.
>
> Such was the beginning of New Minster. This was the first branch which our vine put forth, this the first swarm which came out from our hive. The holy seed took root in the soil, as if cast into the bosom of the fertile earth; it grew into a heap, and from a few grains arose a plenteous crop. For the newly founded house rivalled the fruitfulness of her mother. She conceived and bare three daughters of her own, founding Pipewell, Sawley and Roche.[2]

This story can be found in the Surtees Society's 1862 version of *Memorials of Fountains Abbey*, transcribed by the 19th century scholar J F Walbran, in Latin. The English version above is a translation by Rev J T Fowler from the introduction to the Newminster cartulary.

In Walbran's notes in English, he explains that the original story was written by the chronicler Serlo in about 1207 and also suggests that the earlier account of eight monks, written in Roman numerals as *viii* should perhaps be *xiii*, or thirteen.[3] This was the usual number of monks setting up a new convent, representing Christ and his twelve apostles.

A particular point to note here is the phrase in the extract, *the buildings being set out therein after our manner.* Newminster was established in the correct, standard Cistercian manner.

The third story concerns the destruction of the abbey in its first year. The source of this is Prior Richard of Hexham, written at an uncertain date in the twelfth century:

[1] Prior John, *History of the Church of Hexham*, translated by Joseph Stevenson, 1856, in *The Church Historians of England*, volume 4, part 1, p 12. Also Hodgson, *History of Morpeth*, p 115, in Latin. Also Percy Hedley, *Northumberland Families*, Vol 1, p 196.
[2] J T Fowler, *Newminster Cartulary* introduction, 1876, p ix – x. Original version in Latin, with notes in English, from *Memorials of Fountains Abbey,* transcribed by J T Walbran, Surtees Society Vol 42, 1862, pp 58 - 61
[3] J F Walbran, *Memorials of Fountains Abbey,* Surtees Society Vol 42, 1862, p 58

> While these things were being perpetrated by his followers (1138), the king of Scotland with a considerable force occupied Corbridge. At this period a monastery of the Cistercian rule, founded the same year on the property of Ralph de Merley, was destroyed, and very many others were overwhelmed with the heaviest afflictions.[4]

Before this extract, Prior Richard had described the devastations wrought by the army of the Scottish king David throughout Northumberland during 1138.

The story has spread and been quoted widely. Its origin is probably Hodgson's widely-read *History of Morpeth.* He wrote:

> In the year in which it was built, it was destroyed; and grievous oppressions were committed upon its demesne lands, and the surrounding neighbourhood, by the army of David, king of Scotland.[5]

He followed this with a story about hostile invasions by the Scots in connection with Stannington, which gives an impression that the invasions were continuous. This is very misleading, as the date of this second Stannington story is about 1335, two hundred years after the foundation of Newminster.

Why he put the two stories together like this is a mystery. His source for the quote about David's army is Sir Roger Twysden's *Historiae Anglicanae Scriptores Decem,* written in 1652. Sir Roger Twysden was a baronet and historian, and Rev Joseph Stevenson used this source in 1856 to translate the histories of Hexham by Prior John and Prior Richard. Stevenson makes it clear that Twysden's is the only manuscript copy of these histories:

> … and to which we are indebted for so many important documents connected with the north of England. Twysden's edition is the only copy of the Latin text, and from this source it has been translated.[6]

Hodgson thus must have used the same text.

Another scholar, James Raine, transcribed Prior Richard's history, in Latin, from Twysden's work. He confirms that this is the only known description of the destruction of Newminster.[7]

We must bear in mind that the prior was writing from the perspective of an area which had suffered at the hands of the Scots. David was renowned for founding monasteries not so very far from Newminster, over the border in Scotland. As Prior Richard's is the only source of the story that David's army destroyed the abbey in the first year of its foundation, it needs to be considered with caution.

These three sources together summarise what is known about the earliest origins of Newminster Abbey.

---

[4] Prior Richard, History of the Acts of King Stephen, translated by Joseph Stevenson, 1856, in The Church Historians of England, volume 4, part 1, p 43. Also Hodgson, History of Morpeth, p 115, in Latin.
[5] Rev John Hodgson, History of Morpeth, 1832, p 44
[6] Stevenson, pp vii - viii
[7] James Raine, The Priory of Hexham, 1864, p 79, footnotes

1137 or 1138 or 1139?

There are varying accounts of the year in which the abbey was founded.

Hodgson, page 42, in his *History of Morpeth,* has the monks arriving at Christmas 1138 and the blessing by Geoffrey, Bishop of Durham, as in January 1139.

Prior John of Hexham records that the monks arrived at Morpeth on 5 January 1138, and the Bishop of Durham blessed the abbot Robert the same year.

Prior John and Prior Richard both describe the devastation in Northumberland during 1138 caused by King David of Scotland's armies.

Janet Burton, a historian of the foundation of the British Cistercian houses, has Ranulph de Merlay visiting Fountains Abbey in 1137, and the foundation of Newminster as 1138/9.

This is all further confused by the changing of the system of dates. Until 1751/52, the year ended on 24 March. After that, the new Gregorian calendar was used, with the year starting on 1 January as now.

Writing in his history of the abbots of Newminster in 1915, A M Oliver found the same discrepancies. He used the account from the Memorials of Fountains, with the date of the departure from Fountains as December 1137, and the arrival at Newminster as 5 January 1138.

After much consideration, and not being certain about which historian or transcriber used which system, this account uses the date of January 1138 as being the date of arrival of the monks in Morpeth, and later during 1138 the time when the Scottish army reputedly destroyed the abbey.

Troubled borderlands

Newminster Abbey was founded amidst fighting and devastation in Northumberland. At the castle in Morpeth, the de Merlays must have known and talked about all that was going on in the surrounding countryside, and were probably involved in it. Nevertheless, they were prepared to take all the risks associated with setting up a new monastery.

In the year 1138, any 70 year old man or woman would remember the fearsome events which had taken place in their lifetimes. By the firesides in the humble mud and wattle dwellings of the tied labourers, as well as in the wooden castles of the rulers, stories must have been told of raids and battles, of burned dwellings, raping, slaughter and people being taken away as prisoners.

Older people, who retained good health and a good memory, would be able to talk about the early days following the arrival of the Norman conquerors. They would personally have seen for themselves or at least known about the moving back and forth of the armies as they sought revenge, power and booty. Odo the bishop of Bayeux had ravaged Northumberland in 1080 under orders of William the Conqueror, followed by William's son Robert taking an invading force into Scotland as far as Falkirk. Malcolm III of Scotland had rampaged four times into the county until he was killed near Alnwick by Earl Robert de Mowbray in 1093.

Battles and founding monasteries don't seem to sit comfortably together to the modern mind. Just over the border, in Scotland, Earl David who had become king in 1124 was a French-speaking Norman close to King Henry I. He brought a new civilising way of life to the border valleys of the Teviot and the Tweed. He set up boroughs with markets which encouraged trade; he founded Selkirk Abbey in 1113, moving it to Kelso in 1128. He founded Melrose Abbey in 1136 and Jedburgh in 1138. He and Henry I were good friends, and Henry had married David's sister Matilda.[8] It is possible that the de Merlays knew him. They did the

---

[8] Prior John, p 12

same sort of thing, founding an abbey and taking the first steps in developing the borough of Morpeth.

Immediately after Henry I died in December 1135, David rapidly moved south trying to add Northumberland, Cumberland and Westmorland to his Scottish territories. This was the anarchic period when King Stephen and Henry I's daughter Matilda were in competition for the crown. David sided with Matilda in the dispute and some of the Northumbrian barons, among many other groups from the north of Britain, were with him.

> That infamous army received accessions from the Normans, Germans, and English, from the Northumbrians and Cumbrians, from Teviotdale and Lothian, from the Picts, commonly called Galwegians, and the Scots, and no one knew their number.[9]

Prior John and Prior Richard provide graphic descriptions of the ravages particularly around their own town of Hexham in that year of 1138. But the eastern side of the county was also affected at Wark, Norham and Bamburgh:

> King David then, consigning the siege of Wark to two of the thanes (that is to say his barons) with their retainers, marched with most of his army to the town called Bamborough, where having taken an outwork of the castle he killed nearly a hundred men. And then having destroyed the crops around that place, and around William Bertram's town of Mitford, and in many other parts of Northumberland, he crossed the river Tyne.[10]

It seems entirely likely that Morpeth and the new seedling monastery at Newminster, less than two miles from Mitford, would have suffered. This could be the same episode as the one when Newminster was allegedly destroyed, as described by Prior Richard.

Prior John describes the brutality of the invaders, but at the same time he shows another side to King David.

> These barbarians had no mercy on the infant or the orphan, the aged or the poor; they spared neither sex, age, or rank, nor any degree or profession; they cut to pieces women with child; and, having slain all the males, they next drove off in gangs to Scotland, under the yoke of slavery, the virgins and widows, naked and bound with cords. Nevertheless, the king, as often as they fell to him as a share of the spoil, restored them to Robert, prior of Hexham, in token of their freedom.[11]

Both priors give examples of King David's leniency towards the church. He refused to let his army attack the sanctuary of Hexham abbey, which became a place of safety for many.[12]

In August, King David's army marched south. His seemingly unbeatable army of twenty-six thousand men was defeated by the English under Archbishop Thurstan of York, at what became known as the Battle of the Standard, near Northallerton.[13]

David's army being composed of so many disparate groups must have been hard to control. His concern for sacred premises, such as he had shown at Hexham, suggests that it may not have been under his orders that Newminster was destroyed but rather by uncontrollable elements within his army.

Before the monks arrived
Ranulph's journey to Fountains must have taken place in the years between the foundation of Fountains in 1133 and the arrival of the monks in Morpeth 1138. There was much to

---

[9] Prior Richard, p 43
[10] Prior Richard, p 47
[11] Prior John, p 8
[12] Prior Richard, p 44
[13] Prior Richard, p 47 - 51

organise before the monks could arrive, and Ranulph and the abbot of Fountains would have had considerable interaction.

The buildings which would receive the monks had to be arranged in the correct way, *the buildings being set out therein after our manner.* The Latin wording in the Memorials of Fountains, *et edificiis inibi de more*, is where this originates. The earliest buildings at Newminster, quickly erected, would have been simple constructions probably of timber and clay. The great stone buildings which we might expect to see would be constructed later.

Importantly, the monks of Newminster needed to be granted sufficient land to maintain themselves. If they were to build a church and the many requisite monastic buildings, they needed resources. Land had to be made available and Ranulph and Juliana had to provide it.

Foundation charter

It is very fortunate for us that Newminster's foundation charter has survived. It was a highly important document which would have had to be approved by the abbot of Fountains. It tells us about the first basic land grants to the monks from the de Merlay family.

Newminster's foundation charter, from the Castle Howard Archive.
Reproduced with kind permission of the Hon. Simon Howard

This photograph shows the foundation charter as it is preserved at Castle Howard. It is just about possible to identify the name *Ranulphus de Merlay* at the very beginning of the central section. Its original date was about 1138 and it is possible that this one is a copy of an earlier version. It was written in Latin. Fortunately for us, it has been transcribed and added into the Newminster cartulary by Rev Fowler in 1876. There is also a readily available translation in English for us to look at, in Hodgson's *History of Morpeth*.[14]

---

[14] Hodgson, Morpeth, p 44 in English, p 53 in Latin

Ranulph de Merlay, to all the sons of the holy church, French and English, clergy and laity, present and to come, health:- Know ye that I, with the common consent of my wife and sons, have given in fee and free alms, to the monks of the abbey of Newminster, which I have built, for the health of myself, of my wife, my sons, my lords, and all my friends, and for the souls of my father and mother, my fore-fathers and friends, and of all the faithful that are dead, Rittuna, and whatever belongs to it, in wood or open ground; and part of the wood of Witton, as I set it out to them before my own people; and all the valley between Morpada and Heburn, as the rivulet which is called Fulbecke, runs, and falls into Cottingburn, and as Cottingburn runs under Prestly by a march, which I made to them before my men, as far as the Wenespic, and thus up to the march between me and William Bertram, whatever is there in wood and open land; and on the other side of the water, by the brow of the hill, right across to Lecha, and as Lecha falls into Wdidig, and by Wdidig into Meredene, and by Meredene as far as the Winespic, both in wood and land. And I grant, that they may have free egress for the cattle to the common pasture of all my land; and, at Ulacam, I have given to them, to build their granges upon, from the Eagle's nest to the well of Erard, and as the stream of that well runs into the Lima, and as the Lima runs as far as the march of Forum.[15]

One interesting feature in the first salutation phrase is the mention of both the French and English. This is evidence of a very early charter, where both conquerors and the native notables were in attendance. It carries a sense of neighbourliness between them.

Readers who know Morpeth and the area of mid-Northumberland will recognise some of the place names. First are Rittuna and Witton, which are Ritton and probably Longwitton or Netherwitton. Morpeth and Hebron, the rivulet of Fulbeck and Cottingburn will be easily identified. The Wenespic or Winespic is the Wansbeck river. Ulacam is now called Ulgham, and Lima means the river Lyne. There are places which we don't know now like Lecha, Wdidig and Meredene.

However we can place those we do know on a map, and can see from this that the foundation charter gave lands some miles beyond the town of Morpeth, both to the east and the north west. It would include the abbey site itself and land as far as the march, or boundary, between the de Merlays' land and that of William Bertram, his neighbour in Mitford to the west.

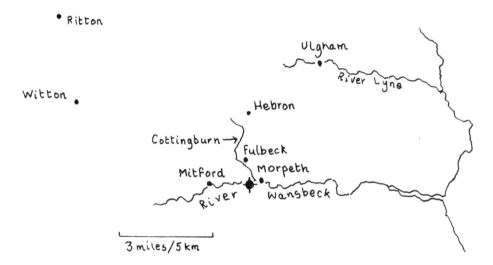

Some of those places in the barony of Morpeth were held by Ranulph de Merlay *in capite,* which means directly from the king.[16] These include Morpeth and the area around Ulgham. Others came from Juliana's side of the marriage.

---

[15] Hodgson, Morpeth, pp 44 - 45
[16] Fowler, Appendix to Newminster cartulary, p 267

There are some typical features of monastic charters which can be seen in this foundation charter, as with the others we will look at later. The salutation comes first and this is usually followed by referring to the benefit of the souls of the donor and his family.

After that, a verbal description of the lands follows. Maps were not used in these early days, so to establish the accuracy of the land grants, various witnesses would perambulate the boundaries described. There are two references to this, in the phrases *as I set it out to them before my own people* and *which I made to them before my men*. We can picture Ranulph's neighbours and family members, and those who would witness the charter, on foot or horseback, making these rounds in three main areas. The first would be locally close to the abbey and around Morpeth, the next in the area around Ulgham and the third further afield around Ritton and Witton.

The monks were granted woodland for timber for their buildings; land for their farms so they could grow cereal crops and pasture the animals; and essential access to the river Wansbeck for the organising of water systems for the abbey. This foundation charter would be the first step in enabling the abbot of Fountains to approve the site for the New Minster, one of his daughter abbeys.

Juliana and her dowry
The story of Newminster seems so much to belong to a man's world. Yet Juliana, English speaking daughter of the Northumbrian Count Cospatric, had an essential part to play in the history of the abbey.

There is a fascinating charter which reveals an agreement between Juliana's father and King Henry I whereby they arrange that she will marry Ranulph de Merlay, and outlines the dowry she will bring with her. This happened a few years before the foundation charter described above and describes the land which Ranulph and Juliana will later donate to Newminster. It is found in the *ancient roll*, the same source as the foundation charter, and it is transcribed in the final pages of the book containing the Newminster cartulary.

Let us picture a group of potentates somewhere in a great hall in Northumberland, around a table. Juliana is there with her mother and other female members of the family. Her father and her brother Edgar are there and at least one of King Henry I's envoys if not the king himself. It is written as if by the king:

> Henricus Rex Angl' et dux Normanniae, justiciariis, vicecomitibus, ministris et omnibus baronibus suis, Francis et Anglis, salutem. Notum sit omnibus vobis me dedisse Ranulpho de Merlay Julianam, filiam comitis Cospatricii, et, per conventionem inter me et patrem suum, dedimus ei in liberum mariale, sibi atque haeredibus suis, scilicet, Horsley, Stanton, Witton, Ritton, Wyndgates, et quandam villam ultra moras …

> Henry, king of England and duke of Normandy, to the justiciaries, vice-counts, ministers and all his barons, French and English, of Northumbria, salutations. Be it known to all of you that I have given to Ranulph de Merlay Juliana, daughter of count Cospatric, and by agreement between me and her father, we have given to her in free marriage, and to her descendants, evidently, Horsley, Stanton, Witton, Ritton, Wyndgates, and a certain village beyond the moors … [17]

The king's permission it seems was required, or at least desirable, before the marriage could take place. Marriages would be arranged between the families of the new Norman barons and the conquered Anglo-Saxon aristocracy. Daughters were useful to create political stability or to further ambitions. As a modern writer explains:

> What heiresses could not do was to marry whom they pleased. A clause in Henry I's coronation charter makes this clear: "If on the death of a baron or other of my men a surviving

---

[17] Monasticon Anglicanum, 1846 edition, Vol 5, Folio item 271-1, p 399. At the Lit and Phil library in Newcastle.
Also Surtees Society Vol 66, 1876, pp 268-269

daughter is the heir I will give her (in marriage) with her land following the advice of my barons.[18]

Thus Juliana, and the package of land which went with her, was part of an arrangement between her father and the king.

There is a further twist to the story. At the end of the marriage agreement quoted above there is another charter with these words from Juliana's brother Edgar:

> Et Edgarus filius Cospatricii comitis confirmavit hanc cartam ut sequitur in haec verba: Edgarus Cospatricii comitis filius omnibus amicis suis, Francis et Anglis, salutem. Sciatis me dedisse et concessisse Julianae sorori meae terram quam meus pater et suus, scilicet comes Cospatricius ei dedit in franco maritagio, et concessit; scilicet, Witton, Horsley, Stanton, Ritton, Windegates, et Leverchilde, cum pertinentiis …

> And Edgar son of count Cospatric confirmed this charter as follows in these words: Edgarus Cospatricii son of the count to all his friends, French and English, greetings. Know that I have given and conceded to Juliana my sister land that my father and hers, namely count Cospatric gave her in free marriage, and conceded, namely, Witton, Horsley, Stanton, Ritton, Windegates, and Leuerchilde, with its appurtenances … [19]

Both charters had many witnesses. Edgar's confirmation charter had a line of eighteen, followed by the words *et multis aliis* which means *many others*. Here are some of them.

> Johanne deacon of Bewick
> Willelmo priest of Stanton
> Ostredo priest of Hartburn
> Alan the cleric
> Grimbauldo de Merlay
> Cospatric son of Leuenoc
> Cospatric of Horsley and Alexander his son
> Godfrid of Wingate[20]

This was an enormous gathering of local notables. If their wives and retainers also attended, it must have been a major occasion. We can't be sure if the king was there or not. Perhaps it was a reason for the king or one of his representatives to gather together all the nobility, French and English, as the conquering families settled in to the local scene.

In this way, Juliana's brother Edgar became part of the agreement of the marriage of his sister. Was that because otherwise he might have inherited, or wanted to inherit, that land himself? With such a list of witnesses, there was no doubt that Juliana's dowry was clearly going to the de Merlay family.

---

[18] Henrietta Leyser, Medieval Women, p 86
[19] Monasticon Anglicanum, p 399 and Surtees Society Vol 66, pp 269
[20] Surtees Society Vol 66, p 269

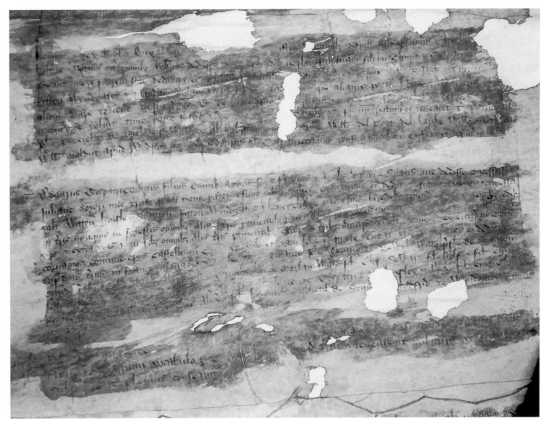

Juliana Cospatric's marriage agreement, from the Castle Howard Archive.
Reproduced with kind permission of the Hon. Simon Howard

The two parts of Juliana and Ranulph's marriage agreement can be seen in the photograph. The first words in the top half are *Henricus Rex Angl' et Dux …*

Two thirds of the way along the second line *Julianam filiam* may be discerned.

In the second part, some of the first sentence is just about readable:
Edgarus Cospatricii comitis filius omnibus amicis suis, Francis et Anglis, salutem. Sciatis me dedisse et concessisse Julianae sorori meae…

Juliana's name is the first word on the second line.

…………………………………………………………………………………………………..

We can at this point make a short chronology of the procedure and the first years of Newminster in the 1130s.

1133	Fountains Abbey established
before 1135	Juliana and Ranulph marriage and dowry agreement with King Henry I
1135	Death of King Henry I
before 1138	Ranulph visited Fountains Abbey Ranulph agreed terms of foundation charter with abbot of Fountains. Site plans agreed. Perhaps some building started
1138	Monks arrive from Fountains with Robert who is blessed as abbot by Geoffrey, bishop of Durham, about the feast of Epiphany, 5 January
1138	Alleged destruction of the earliest abbey buildings by army of King David of Scotland

Newminster's place in the Cistercian expansion

Ranulph de Merlay chose the Cistercian order for his new monastery. The order had started in 1106 at Citeaux in France. The monks there had chosen to move away from the earlier Cluniac abbey at Molesme in order to pursue the stricter way of life as originally expounded by St Benedict in the sixth century. The Cistercians were known as *white monks,* from their garments of undyed white wool, which distinguished them from the earlier Benedictines who wore black. It attracted followers quickly and in 1113 a second monastery was established at La Ferte, another at Pontigny in 1114 and two more at Morimond and Clairvaux in 1115. By 1119, another five were completed and the Cistercian Order was formally established.

We can see from this how quickly the movement spread. By 1153 there were 339 Cistercian monasteries within the order, rising to 525 by the end of the century. They stretched from Scotland to Poland, and the number continued to rise.

The first Cistercian monastery in England was founded at Waverley in 1128, the next at Rievaulx in March 1132, and Fountains in December 1132. At first the monks of Fountains had followed the Benedictine rule and they settled among the rocks and caves of the valley of the river Skell. Shortly afterwards they sought and obtained permission to join the Cistercian order.

Things moved very quickly. There is a little bit of a debate about which exactly was the first daughter house of Fountains, owing to how this is defined; but Newminster was certainly a candidate, the others being at Haverholme in Lincolnshire and Kirkstead in Lincolnshire.

In his book *Fountains Abbey* historian Glyn Coppack described the foundation of Newminster:

> A colony was dispatched to the wilds of Northumberland under the abbacy of Robert, the ex-Whitby monk who was one of the first Fountains community. The name given to this new daughter-house is significant for it was called *Novum Monasterium* or Newminster, the original name of Citeaux. Its temporary buildings were laid out by Abbot Robert himself 'after our manner' though the founder, Ranulph de Merlay, lord of Morpeth, claimed responsibility for their construction. This split responsibility was to ensure that suitable buildings were erected before the new colony arrived, a requirement of Cistercian statutes since at least 1113.[21]

Coppack thus confirms that Abbot Robert had started to lay out the buildings before 1138, when the party of monks arrived at Morpeth castle. It seems likely that Robert had visited beforehand.

Newminster itself followed the pattern of creating daughter houses in its turn, and within a decade established three new abbeys at Pipewell in 1143, Roche in 1147 and Sawley in 1147.[22]

What were the Cistercian monks trying to achieve? An English monk, Stephen Harding, became the abbot at Citeaux and was largely responsible for establishing a new monastic way of life. His teachings included the *Carta Caritas,* the Charter of Love, which was the order's constitution. There were several important principles.

- Poverty and a simple life
- Separation from the outside world
- Self-sufficiency without income from churches or other revenue
- Land-based economy

---

[21] Glyn Coppack, Fountains Abbey, Amberley, 2009, pp 12 - 30
[22] Janet Burton, The foundation of the British Cistercian Houses, in Cistercian Art and Architecture in the British Isles, ed Christopher Norton, Cambridge University Press, 1986, p 397

The monks were to divide their time between prayer, manual labour and reading. To enable them to serve God in the intended way, a large labour force and many acres of land were required. One of the Cistercians' special innovations was the creation of a secondary level of monks who would do much of the manual work. The *choir monks* were the highest layer of the system, the reason for the existence of the monastery. Beneath them was a lower grade of brethren known as *conversi,* or *lay brothers.* They were to be accommodated in a distinct part of the monastery with separate eating, sleeping and washing arrangements. Their lower status was ensured by their not being allowed to have books, or to learn anything except the Paternoster, Credo and a few other prayers.[23] The whole of the expansion of the Cistercian system, including that at Newminster in the north east of England, relied on this two-layer arrangement.

Newminster would play a particularly important role in the north of England. It was among the most important abbeys between Yorkshire and Scotland and the only Cistercian one. Just over the border in Scotland were King David's foundations of Kelso, Melrose and Jedburgh, founded by 1138. Dryburgh was founded around 1150 by Hugh de Moreville.

Archaeologist Barbara Harbottle made this comment:

> From a local point of view, Newminster was of considerable importance in a county that contained only five independent monasteries (excluding cells, nunneries and friaries) ... and just three Cistercian houses in the four northernmost English counties, the other two being Holm Cultram and Calder in Cumberland.[24]

Newminster would become one of the great wool-producing Cistercian abbeys of the day, managing land from the Cheviot heights to the North Sea. As the bird flies this is a distance of about 35 miles and it comprised thousands of acres. Like Fountains, Rievaulx and Melrose, the abbey managed a vast estate from its central location next to Morpeth.

The twelve or more monks had first to settle in to their new surroundings, on their piece of cultivated land between the river and the woodlands.

---

[23] Newminster Cartulary footnote, p 120
[24] Harbottle, p 92

2 The New Minster

The first and later buildings

The New Minster was built within a meander of the river Wansbeck, a flattish riverside area known locally as a *haugh*. It was surrounded by steep banks on three sides, with the river forming the fourth. Its situation was ideal; quiet but not remote. The de Merlay castle lay a quarter of a mile away with the little settlement of Morpeth sheltering in its shadow.

What did the monks do when they arrived? How did they establish themselves? They needed temporary accommodation and a reliable water supply. It is all so long ago, and information is very difficult to find. Through English Heritage, I was able to receive help from Cistercian expert archaeologist and historian Glyn Coppack. Much of what follows is gleaned from email communications as well as his invaluable book *Fountains Abbey*.

We have no details about the first temporary buildings at Newminster but we can draw inferences from Fountains. Coppack explains:

> What was provided was a new timber monastery built to the model already provided at Clairvaux, and on a new site. According to the statutes of the order, this would comprise an oratory, a dormitory, a refectory, a chamber for guests, and a porter's lodge, the most basic provision necessary for monastic life. No cloister was included, and these buildings were intended to serve only until the community achieved stability and could afford to build permanent buildings in stone.[25]

An experienced monk called Geoffroi de Ainai had been sent from Clairvaux, the principal site of the Cistercian order in France, to assist the monks at Fountains. Robert, the new abbot of Newminster, had been trained by Geoffroi de Ainai at Fountains. It is likely that Robert would have visited Ranulph de Merlay to check over the proposed site in the years between 1133 and 1138.

Were Newminster's first temporary buildings similar to those of Fountains? Coppack has this to say:

> It is interesting to note that Fountains did not subsequently use the Clairvaux layout for the temporary buildings of its own daughter houses … Abbot Robert of Newminster, the other monk trained by Geoffroi, chose to build two great aisled buildings at Sawley (Salley) when he established his first daughter house there in 1147 and both of these buildings have been located by excavation. It would appear that there was a steady development in the planning of temporary buildings … In every case where such buildings are documented, they are described as being 'according to the custom of the order'.[26]

From this it is at least possible to surmise that Newminster may have originally consisted of two great aisled buildings, as at Sawley, the walls of which walls were of mud or clay, stiffened with slight timbers.[27]

Soon after moving into their temporary buildings, which as we know were prepared by Ranulph de Merlay, the monks started on their first stone church.

This would have been started in the 1140s. It was similar to that being constructed at Fountains at around the same time. In style, it was typical of the Cistercian order's early churches which were buildings of great simplicity. It was cruciform, or cross-shaped, in design, with a short square-ended presbytery at the east end to house the altar. It had small rectangular transept chapels in the arms of the cross. These features can be seen in the plan which follows.

---

[25] Coppack, p 21
[26] Coppack, pp 25 - 26
[27] Coppack, p 26

At Fountains, the first stone church was constructed around the temporary wooden church which was deemed to have great spiritual importance. It is not out of the question that the same happened at Newminster although this is only speculation.

The basic shape of the church remained unchanged although it underwent rebuilding on a larger scale around 1160. All the other buildings which a monastery required were gradually erected, reflecting the typical Cistercian plan which can be seen at other monastic sites like Fountains or Roche to this day. What did the complex of buildings look like and what can they tell us about the lives of those within the precinct walls? To get some answers, we'll look at the report by Barbara Harbottle and Peter Salway, produced after excavations between 1961 and 1963.[28]

Harbottle explains the conclusions she drew about the dating of the complex:

> The abbey was in the course of building for a number of years, from the second half of the twelfth century well into the thirteenth. It seems likely that the church, cloister, and west and east ranges date from before 1200, and the rere-dorter and south range from the thirteenth century. The chapter house was probably enlarged in the latter part of the thirteenth century, and the galilee and some at least of the buttresses on the church may well have been added as late as the fifteenth century.[29]

The excavations concentrated on the central monastic buildings including the church, the chapter house, the cloister and the domestic living spaces. From the plan we can see the church as the most obvious feature. The cloister lies to the south. The east range of buildings contained the area in which the choir monks lived. The west range was the premises of the lay brothers.

These east and west ranges were to cater for the two levels of hierarchy specific to Cistercian monasteries, the choir monks and the lay brothers. The choir monks kept to the enclosed inner sanctum of church and cloister. The lay brothers lived in a sort of half-way house between the choir monks and the outer world. Their job was to see to the abbey's lands. They attended daily services at the church when they were not out working on the farms but were limited to the rear western section of the nave behind a screen.

We can see from the plan that the cross-shaped church is the largest and most important building. At the western end is the entrance, through a small porch known as a galilee. The long nave faces east. Half way along was the screen, and beyond that the seating for the choir monks, spelled *quire* on the plan. Next was the crossing with the transepts on each side and finally the presbytery at its end.

The monks would enter and leave the church from the south transept which gave access to their quarters. Under the sheltered arcades of the cloister the monks would read and meditate. There would be a garden within the cloister square.

Following the typical Cistercian pattern, next to the south transept was a library, a sacristy where the sacred vessels and vestments of the church were held. Beyond that was the chapter house. In this room, daily meetings would take place where the abbey's business was conducted, discipline enforced, and a chapter of the Rule of St Benedict read out.

Beyond the chapter house was a small room called a parlour where the monks were allowed to talk. After a narrow passage was the substantial building on the first floor of which was the monks' dormitory, here called a *dorter*. Below that was the undercroft, a large space devoted to a range of different activities. To the rear of the dormitory was the *rere dorter,* or toilet block, and a drain.

---

[28] Harbottle, Barbara and Salway, Peter, *Excavations at Newminster Abbey, Northumberland, 1961 – 1963*, Archaeologia Aeliana, 4th Series, Vol 42, 1964
[29] Harbottle, p 95

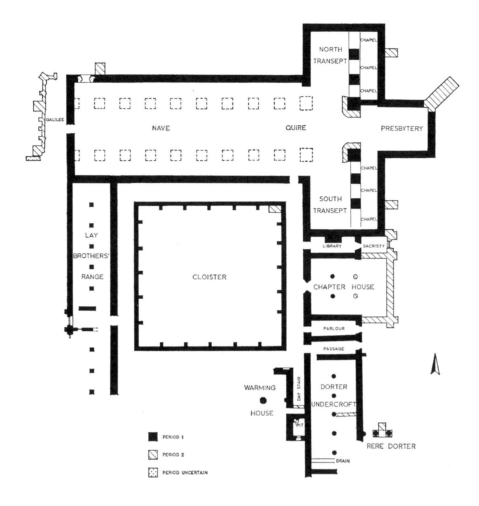

*The plan of the monastic core produced by Barbara Harbottle and
Peter Salway after excavations in 1961, 1962 and 1963*

With thanks to the Society of Antiquaries of Newcastle upon Tyne

There is no evidence in Harbottle's plan of the location of the refectory, the large room where
the monks ate their meals in silence. From other Cistercian sites we can guess that it
probably was on the south side of the cloister, along with the kitchen, and this is confirmed
by its surviving earthworks. There is a warming house marked, the only place where there
would have been any heating. If the fire was allowed, it was lit from All Saints' Day on 1
November until Good Friday the following spring.

Because a plan does not show us what the buildings themselves looked like, there are some
obvious questions. Did the church have a visible and striking tower? And how high was the
church? One, two or three elevations? Also, what were the architectural details of the
windows and doorways?

Coppack has this to tell us:

> The first design at Newminster had no crossing tower, and neither did the contemporary
> churches at Rievaulx and Fountains. Fountains changed the design of its crossing in the mid-
> late 1150s, and inserted a tower. At Newminster the one crossing pier we know about is
> certainly an addition designed specifically to carry a tower, and that must go with the rebuilding
> of the eastern arcade in the 1180s.[30]

---

[30] Coppack, email to author, November 2013, quoted with permission.

The tower spire at Fountains is likely to have had a 60 degree pitch, and this would have been similar at Newminster.[31]

Was Newminster's church a several-storey high building, such an impression as we might have in our heads after a visit to Fountains or Roche?

> The important point is that the nave was not rebuilt when the transepts were in the 1170s or 1180s, so it is unlikely that the transepts had three-storey elevation like Roche. Roche had high vaults, but that goes with the three-storey elevation. The lack of ribs from a high vault at Newminster confirms that the nave and transepts did not have high stone vaults but retained their traditional wooden roofs. I think the church maintained its high timber roofs until the suppression.[32]

On the question of architectural style, Coppack tells us:

> The detailing is Gothic but the windows and doors remain round-headed. There was probably a late medieval re-windowing of the church, especially the gable walls, for which there is a lot of Perpendicular window tracery lying about the site.

> Newminster would also have had the same sort of rose windows as Rievaulx in both the east and west gables.

By *Gothic*, he means a style in which the arches and windows were pointed, dating from the later 12th century, rather than rounded as in earlier times. *Perpendicular* refers to a style from roughly 1350 onwards.

And his final memorable words:

> The early church at Newminster would have been very similar in appearance to those at Rievaulx and Fountains, a great barn-like building.

The abbey church on the cover illustration of this book by Victor Ambrus is the result of close co-ordination between him and Coppack.

In 2011, a new study of Newminster's site was commissioned by the North East Civic Trust and undertaken by Archaeological Research Services Ltd from Gateshead. This didn't involve actual excavations but used non-intrusive surveying methods. The consultants' report contains plans, text and photographs, including architectural details of the remaining stonework of the church, cloister and chapter house. It is well worth reading.

The survey included the central site excavated by Harbottle, but extended over a wider area showing the location of other buildings and features. The plans show a likely cemetery to the north of the church and another possible one to the east. An infirmary lay to the south east of the church. Its associated chapel has an unexcavated tiled pavement. The building in the extreme south east corner is considered likely to be the abbot's lodging.

There was a range of buildings on the west of the site containing guest accommodation, granary, brewery and other industrial buildings. To the north may have been the site of corrodians' houses, of people from outside the abbey but who lived in association with it.

In the east of the site was to be found what the archaeologists suggest could be the home grange, the closest farm to the actual monastery, and a mill with its pond.[33]

---

[31] Coppack, email to author
[32] Coppack, email to author
[33] Archaeological Research Services Ltd (ARS Ltd), Archaeological Survey at Newminster Abbey, Morpeth, Northumberland, 2011, pp 66 and 73, figures 94 and 102

The survey also shows that Ranulph de Merlay chose the site for the monastery on fields which were under cultivation. It was not a wilderness of scrub and bog. There is a pattern of ridge and furrow, some of which is overlain by the monastic buildings:

As a group, the furlongs (ridge and furrow) seem to be arranged so as to respect the centre of the site implying that there could be an earlier settlement, or monastic settlement, there.[34]

Perhaps the earlier settlement is referring to the first phase of the site, when the temporary buildings were in place.

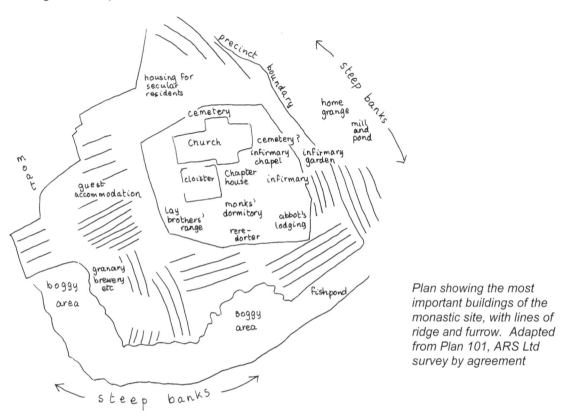

Plan showing the most important buildings of the monastic site, with lines of ridge and furrow. Adapted from Plan 101, ARS Ltd survey by agreement

The monastery's water supply

The Cistercians were experts at water management. Newminster needed a steady supply to provide sanitation, for the kitchen, and for all the industrial processes including milling, brewing and blacksmithing. For this, the planners would need to divert water from a nearby river. Anyone who has visited abbeys such as Fountains or Melrose will be familiar with the stone-lined channels through which the water was diverted.

Newminster's water supply is not thoroughly understood. In the plan which follows, details in its eastern half are extracted from the ARS Ltd report.[35] A possible water course, they indicate, may have come in to the monastic complex from the west and then turned south into a moat. This moat looks as if it would have connected with what is now a boggy area a little further south. This was crossed by an earthwork which may have acted as a dam.

There is a suggestion in the archaeologists' survey that "it is just possible that the dam provided the platform for an aqueduct to carry water from a spring head (or heads) on the natural scarp to the south into the monastic interior".[36] If so, this would have been the site's drinking water supply, kept separate from channels for sanitation and industrial use. On the bank just south of the boggy area they identified a well which on older maps is marked as *Abbey Well*.

---

[34] ARS Ltd, p 81 and plan 101
[35] ARS Ltd, figures 101, 102, 104
[36] ARS Ltd, p 85

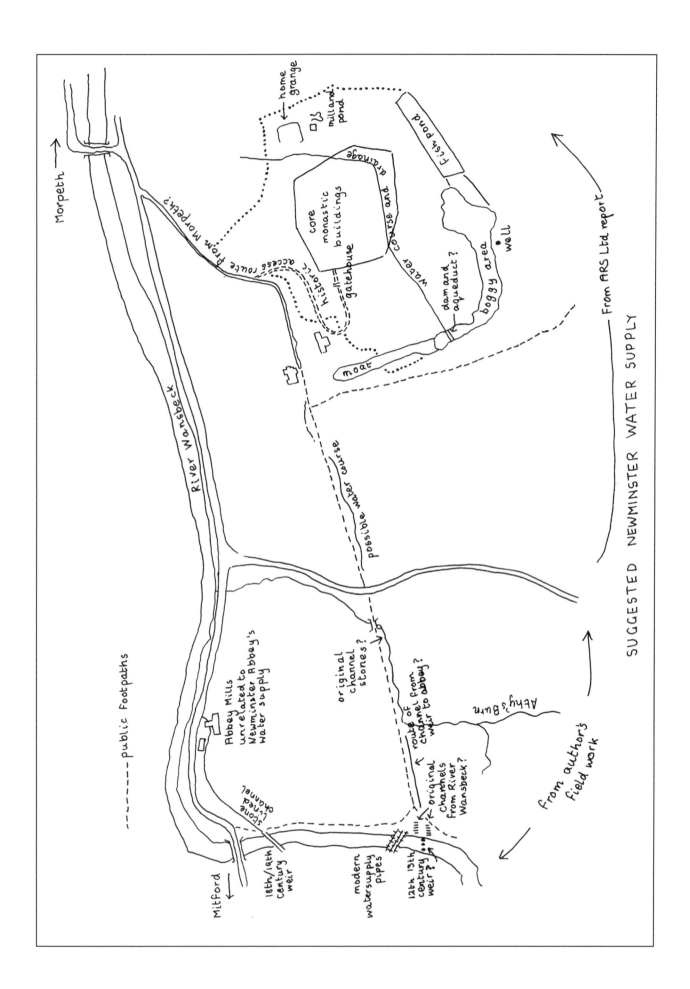

SUGGESTED NEWMINSTER WATER SUPPLY

— — — public Footpaths

Morpeth

River Wansbeck

Mitford

18th/19th century weir?

stone lined channel

Abbey Mills unrelated to Newminster Abbey's water supply

original channel stones?

route of channel from weir to abbey?

Athy's Burn

original channels from River Wansbeck?

modern water supply pipes

12th/13th century weir?

From author's field work

possible water course

home grange

mill and pond

core monastic buildings

historic access route from Morpeth

gatehouse

water course and drainage

moat

dam and aqueduct?

boggy area

well

Fish pond

From ARS Ltd report

South of the dam the water would be led into what was probably the fish pond. This low-lying curve of land occupies an ancient channel of the river and present-day vegetation still shows that it is a wetland. The archaeologists suggest that the water was managed to run through this area, serving the fish pond and on to a mill before continuing to the Wansbeck.[37]

The report also shows that a water course may have led from the dam through the central monastic buildings.[38] The lay brothers' and the choir monks' dormitories, as well as the kitchen areas, would need a flowing water system. The usual pattern in Cistercian monasteries was for the toilet areas of the dormitories to be at the rear, over a running water course. If the kitchen at Newminster lay between these two dormitory blocks, the course of this channel would deal with that as well.

The main water course and drainage would have needed a strong and reliable supply. The boundary of the archaeologists' survey area didn't go far enough west to show how water from the river Wansbeck might have arrived at the site, and so a nearby resident and former geography teacher, Rod Mathieson, and I did a little field work. The results of that are in the western part of the plan shown here.

We had a few clues to start us off. Rev Fowler, in his introduction to the Newminster cartulary, writing in 1878, wrote the following:

> The great sewer for sanitary purposes, which also turned two or three mills, was an artificial watercourse taken off from the Wansbeck about a mile and a half higher up, where a weir or dam was put across. This watercourse can still be traced through a considerable part of its length, and for some distance contains a briskly running stream of surface drainage. In a wood near the river it is now dry (the weir having long disappeared), and it retains its bank of out-thrown material, reminding one of a Roman agger and fosse. Near the abbey it was conveyed in an arched conduit of stone about five or six feet high; this has been destroyed within the last few years, together with the original oak frame of the sluice by which the admission of water was regulated.[39]

Rod and I started our investigations at the site on the bottom left of the plan, near where three huge pipes taking water from Fontburn Reservoir south to Bedlington and Tynemouth cross the river. Just to the south of the pipes are two clearly dug channels leading out from the river bank. This seems to be the area described by Fowler as like a Roman agger and fosse. After some disturbance, probably caused by work for the water pipes, the channel leads eastwards towards the monastery. Before following the channel, we looked down at the river itself.

Everyone in Morpeth remembers the horrific floods of 2008. Among other damage, the concreted weir a little further downstream from this point was destroyed. This weir is probably a couple of hundred years old and held the river behind it in a deep pond-like state for a good quarter of a mile. Now that the weir is destroyed, the river is flowing in a more natural way. It has become shallow and after the dry summer of 2013 particularly so. To our surprise, Rod and I discovered what we feel is very likely to be relics of the original weir of the Newminster monks. We could see a broad line of stones, some of them cut stones, extending half way across the river bed. Next to it, there were many large, cut stones lying in the river bed and in the bank. At the time when Rev Fowler wrote, and until the floods of 2008, all this would have been under the water.

---

[37] ARS Ltd survey, p 87
[38] ARS Ltd survey, figure 102
[39] Fowler, p xv

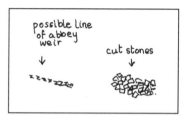

Very pleased with our discovery, we next followed the channel in the direction of the monastery. Behind heavy overgrowth, we could see the ditch which the channel had now become. At the first field junction Athy's Burn ran into the ditch. In wet weather, this stream bubbles and gurgles along, Rev Fowler's briskly running stream, but this day it was a mere trickle. We both felt that Athy's Burn probably would have been diverted by the monks to join the channel from the Wansbeck to increase the supply. We were really hoping to find some stonework along the course of the ditch, although it was likely to have been robbed during the last centuries. We couldn't see any stonework through the dense vegetation, and agreed we'd need to return when it had died back. But then, just as we reached the bridge where the stream was diverted north towards the Wansbeck, we saw them – cut stonework partly hidden by vegetation on the north side of the bank of the stream. This seemed miraculous! There were three rows of stonework extending about two metres in length, before it disappeared under plantlife and silt.

Crossing the road we entered the area which had been surveyed by the archaeologists where an indicative channel was described in their text as *a potential water course*.[40] It led easterly until, as they suggest, it could have been diverted south into the moat.

---

[40] ARS Ltd survey, p 87, and figure 104

As for the arched conduit of stone and the sluice near the abbey, referred to by Rev Fowler, nothing of this has shown up in the ARS Ltd survey of 2011.

Thus the archaeologists' survey supplemented with our fieldwork seems to show the basis for the water system which served the monastery. It all needs a lot more work and excavation.

Abbey Mills are not Newminster Abbey's mills

Rod Mathieson lives at Mill House, Abbey Mills, on the road between Morpeth and Mitford. There are several houses in this cluster. From the mid-18th century and well into the 20th, there were two mills here. The first was a woollen mill. The second one was at various times a cornmill and a sawmill. The weir which can be seen from the nearby road bridge was destroyed by the floods in 2008. The water channel which runs from there through to the mills is now consequently dry. We both agree that this mill system is not the one that serviced the monastery despite confusion caused by the name of the properties there.

The channel leading towards the mills from the weir is lined with good quality stonework, although it is being severely damaged by trees and plants as no-one is maintaining it. Where did the stones come from? It seems distinctly possible that stones from the nearby abbey channel, obsolete at the time the later mills were constructed, would have been used. Further investigations are needed.

Shepherd boy with a lay brother, near the abbey in the year 1200.
Illustration by Victor Ambrus. Church design guided and authorised by Cistercian expert Glyn Coppack

3   The cartulary

Monks, builders, carters and shepherds

Let us now lift up that mantle of scrub-laden turf from the mounds in the spring-green field where the ruins of Newminster lie buried. The images of the abbey and its busy inhabitants can re-form before our eyes. Through the gateway in the precinct wall are passing ox-drawn carts driven by local peasants taking in the timber and building materials. Lay brothers in their brown habits are helping to unload the goods. Some are working in the garden; others are hammering in the workshops and baking the bread. Some are feeding the fish; others sweeping the dormitories and cleaning the kitchen. Water from the dam is gurgling along the drainage channels and the mill wheels are turning.

The white-clad choir monks are ambling in the cloister, reading and meditating; others are writing in the scriptorium or consulting the charters in the library. At mealtimes, they make their way to the lavatorium where they wash their hands before sitting down to a silent meal, listening to the daily reading. Eight times every twenty-four hours they make their way to the church where they perform their offices.

While all this is going on, the stone masons are at work gradually completing the church and the monks' living quarters; cutting and shaping stone, mixing mortar, carrying loads up ladders into the scaffolding. There is noise and hammering and orders are being called.

In the fields adjoining the buildings peasants are ploughing and sowing, the women caring for the children as well as helping in the fields. Shepherd lads are looking after the sheep and the new-born lambs. Some of these people are the families of the lay brothers. To them, the abbey remains a mysterious enclosure behind the precinct walls. Only a few of the men will pass through in the course of their labours; the women never.

There is movement along all the roadways leading to the abbey; carts are moving to Blyth for loads of coal and salt; others under special guard are bringing the communion wine from the dock on the Tyne; shepherds are moving the flocks to and from the outer farms.

On occasions, a king of England would approach the abbey with his entourage, even at times his army. As they unload there is the clatter of armour and the rustle of expensive fabrics. The privileged guests will be entertained by the abbot and accommodated in the special buildings in the outer close. The monks and the lay brothers have all the hustle and bustle of preparing for the important visitors and the expense of feeding them and their animals.

On special saints' days, St Katherine's in particular on 29 April, the poor of Morpeth and the surrounding countryside gather outside the gateway,where they are given oatcakes and herrings. They don't get through the doors.

This is a busy landscape. For the first century and a half after its foundation, Newminster was enjoying its golden age. The church and stone buildings were gradually being completed and much of the surrounding countryside for miles in every direction was being absorbed into one great agricultural complex. There would be various ebbings and flowings, contractions and expansions, but the abbey thrived. Newminster was at the heart of life in central Northumberland. And yet so little has survived to tell us what went on.

Chartularium Abbatiae de Novo Monasterio

But we do have one important document – Newminster's cartulary, its collection of charters.

From the earliest days, the monks at Newminster carefully stored all their charters on rolls or on small pieces of vellum or parchment. These legal agreements between themselves and various donors gave them the right to use land for their farms or to move across the land of others. They might have to agree a fee for this or sometimes the donors relinquished payment. The charters described the terms of the agreement. There were no maps so, as we saw in the foundation charter, the boundaries would be described verbally. Often the charters were confirmed years or a generation or two later. The monks did not own the land in the modern sense, but had the right to use it. As the years passed by, it was a good idea to confirm the original rights.

There were excellent reasons for giving grants to the monastery; the donors would be accorded the prayers of the monks for the benefit of their souls and those of their ancestors and descendants thus reducing their time in purgatory; they might be buried in the abbey church bringing them similar benefits after death; and there could be income from the rent. Over the decades more and more charters were written and it became usual for abbeys to organise them into one single document:

> As the numbers of grants increased, it became ever more difficult to store the accumulated rolls of charters so that they were accessible when needed. By the eleventh century, the greater monasteries were finding it imperative to devise some more efficient form of filing the information, and the practice developed of compiling land registers or cartularies which could be kept up to date as further gifts accrued.[41]

The earliest of Newminster's charters which survived the process of being copied into the cartulary did not often contain the date. It was not until 1274 that charters were dated. Legal historian Theodore Plucknett explains:

> Before the reign of Edward I it is unusual to find the deed dated, but from the fourteenth century the sealing and witness clause are replaced by a dating clause, announcing the time and place.[42]

To get help with dates for the earlier charters, I've had to consult the family trees of the donor families, and these can be seen in the appendices to this book.

None of the original charters has survived but the cartulary somehow did. It had an adventurous journey, and a lucky escape. It doesn't seem to have been available in 1832 when Hodgson was writing his history of Morpeth. He used a great variety of sources in his writings about Newminster but nowhere as far as I've seen does he actually quote it:

> The chartulary, containing copies of the evidences of this house, was in the possession of lord William Howard, when Doddsworth, in 1638, made his extracts from it, printed by Dugdale.[43]

He is referring to the *Monasticon Anglicanum* which was originally compiled by historians Roger Dodsworth and William Dugdale in the reign of King Charles I. At the library of the Literary and Philosophical Society in Newcastle there are seven or eight volumes of a 19th century upgraded version of the *Monasticon Anglicanum* and you can go and see them.[44]

This story has the Surtees Society to thank for its access to the cartulary. The society was founded in Durham in 1834 and its purpose was to publish historic texts. In 1876, it decided to have the Newminster cartulary transcribed. Rev J T Fowler, a brilliant scholar who gets

---

[41] James Bond, Monastic Landscapes, Tempus, 2004, pp 14 - 16

[42] Theodore Plucknett, A Concise History of the Common Law, Liberty Fund, 1929 and 1956, p 612

[43] Hodgson, Morpeth, p 44

[44] Caley, Ellis and Bandinell, 1846, Monasticon Anglicanum by Dodsworth and Dugdale, Vol 5, folio item 271-1

many a mention in this story, undertook the work. In his introduction to the book he describes its adventurous journey:

> This MS. was long supposed to be lost, but Mr Woodman of Morpeth, knowing that Mr. Edw. Cook of Blakemoor, a well-known antiquary and barrister, who died about the end of the last century, had a great collection of MSS., made enquiry among his descendants and found the MS. in the possession of Mr. Burn of Southwick near Sunderland, who sold it to the late Lord Carlisle for £10. It has been lent to the Surtees Society in order that the present edition might be printed from the original MS., which is contained in one volume consisting of 155 leaves of vellum in vellum covers, size 8¼ inches by 5½. It has been injured by too free an application of galls, which has rendered many portions almost illegible; nevertheless it is hoped that all has been deciphered correctly.[45]

Fowler's transcription of the Newminster cartulary was titled *Chartularium Abbathiae de Novo Monasterio*. It was published in 1878 as Volume 66.[46] He transcribed it in the original Latin but he wrote a useful introduction in English, adding marginal notes in English in the main body of the text from time to time. It doesn't seem ever to have been fully translated. Later historians used Fowler's transcriptions to translate only the parts of it which they required.

As well as transcribing the cartulary, another document had survived along with it. Fowler appended this to his Volume 66, entitling it *Portion of an Ancient Roll*. The foundation charter described in the previous chapter was found in the *ancient roll:*

> This charter has never been entered in the cartulary. It is here printed from the ancient roll which is referred to in Dugdale, *Mon. Angl.* vol. v. p. 399 (last ed.), where it is printed as from this roll, but not quite accurately … the roll is unfortunately incomplete at both ends. In its present state it consists of seven skins sewn together, and is 12 ft. 2 in. long by 10 ½ in. broad. The first skin is much decayed.[47]

Fowler thus inserted the foundation charter into its rightful chronological place when he transcribed the cartulary, even though it was from a different source.

Juliana's marriage agreement to Ranulph de Merlay was also recorded in the *ancient roll.*

When he had finished, Fowler returned the original cartulary and the *ancient roll* to the Howards, the family of the Earl of Carlisle who inherited much of the de Merlay lands. And there they rest in their box, together with a copy of the Surtees Society transcription, in the archives of Castle Howard in North Yorkshire. The archivist explained that the box had arrived at Castle Howard from Lord William Howard's library at Naworth Castle in Cumbria, although the exact date is not known.

It is the most important source of information about the abbey and fundamental to this story.

---

[45] Fowler, p xi
[46] Chartularium Abbathiae de Novo Monasterio, the Newminster Cartulary, Surtees Society Vol 66, 1876, transcribed Rev J T Fowler. It is also available at www.archives.org
[47] Fowler, p 2 and p 277

The box containing the ancient roll and the Newminster cartulary. The Surtees Society transcription of 1876 lies underneath.

From the Castle Howard Archive. Reproduced with kind permission of the Hon. Simon Howard

CHARTULARIUM ABBATHIÆ DE NOVO MONASTERIO.

————◦◦⫷❃⫸◦◦————

RANULPHUS DE MERLAY omnibus sanctæ ecclesiæ filiis, Francis, Anglicis, clericis et laicis, præsentibus et futuris, salutem. Sciatis me communi consilio et consensu uxoris meæ et puerorum meorum, dedisse in feudo et in elemosinam monachis Abbathiæ Novi Monasterii quam ego ipse construxi pro salute mea et uxoris meæ et puerorum meorum et dominorum meorum et omnium antecessorum meorum et pro animabus patris et matris meæ, parentum et amicorum meorum cuntorumque fidelium defunctorum, Rittunam et quicquid ad illam pertinet, et in bosco et in plano, et partem silvæ de Wittuna sicut eis coram meis hominibus divisi, et totam vallem inter Morpada et Milford (*sic*), videlicet ex una parte aquæ a recta divisa inter Morpada et Hebre, et sicut currit rivulus qui vocatur Fulebek, et cadit in Cottingburna, et sicut currit Cottingburna subtus Prestley per unam divisam quam eis coram meis hominibus feci usque in Wenespic, et sic usque ad divisam inter me et Willelmum Bertram, quicquid ibi est in bosco et in plano, et ex altera parte aquæ per ipsum supercilium montis ex transverso usque ad unum lecha (*sic*), et sicut illa lecha vadit usque Wdedig, et per Wdedig usque Merdene, et per Merdene usque in Wenespic, et silvam et terram. Et concedo ut habeant liberum exitum pecuniæ¹ suæ ad communem pasturam tocius terræ meæ. Et apud Wlacam ad construendas grangias suas dedi eis a nido aquilæ usque ad fontem Egardi, et (*sicut*) currit rivulus ejusdem fontis in Linam,

Carta prima.

Ranulph de Merlay, the builder of Newminster.

Ritton, Witton, and valley between Morpeth and Mitford.

The Wansbeck.

Ulgham: the Eagle's nest and Egard's Well.

The first page of the Surtees Society's transcription of the Newminster cartulary. This is the foundation document which was taken from the ancient roll, seen above

With thanks to the Society of Antiquaries of Newcastle upon Tyne

34

Newminster's filing system

A lovely green-bound hardback copy of the Surtees Society's volume 66 from 1876, in Latin, was on my desk as I prepared to write this story. How was I going to tackle it?

Once I'd read the introduction and skimmed through the marginal notes, I took a deep breath. First, I listed the places named within it, most of which are still recognisable despite the variety of spellings. Then, as I looked more carefully, I could see that the hundreds of charters were in sections. They were labelled Gradus II, Gradus III and Gradus IV. Also, from time to time, a section was marked as *locus vij* or similar. What did *gradus* mean? Or *locus*? In one of his marginal notes, Fowler enlightened me:

> It would seem as if the original documents were arranged in 'pigeon-holes' numbered to correspond with marginal numbers in the cartulary, these 'pigeon holes' in *gradus* or rows one above another, and these perhaps in *loci* or divisions of some kind.[48]

I began to realise that Newminster's charters were organised in a double system of donor families and geographical areas. The first few *gradus* (the word is both singular and plural) were given over to charters from the important families. Within each *gradus* the charters were arranged according to places. Within those sections the filing clerk would presumably put the charters in date order although very few were dated, especially in the earlier days. This system was obviously logical to him but it can be very tricky for the modern reader.

A problem was that there are so many Rogers and Williams in the first generations of the de Merlay and Bertram families that trying to work out who did what, and when, was very difficult. Many of the charters did not specify whether they were from Roger I, Roger II or Roger III. This was made more difficult because although the system was more or less chronological within each *gradus* or *locus*, this was not always the case.

In the end, I cut out lots of little squares of paper, one for each of the relevant charters for the sections I wanted to work on, and put them in order myself, working out which was Roger I or Roger II or Roger III using clues such as *proavi mea* for *my great grandfather*. I relied heavily on Percy Hedley's family trees in his book *Northumberland Families*, which you can see in the appendices to this book. Finally, I stapled my little squares onto larger sheets.

By the time I had done this I felt I knew the mind of the monks. I was sharing their understanding of where things were, and how the system worked. If for example the abbot needed to refer to the records it would be easy for the monk to pull the relevant ones out. This is exactly what happened at one time in a year between 1239 and 1265, when the abbot wanted Roger Bertram III to confirm the thirteen previous charters which went back two hundred years to the time of his great great grandfather William Bertram, the first baron of Mitford:

> Roger filius Rogeri Bertram de Mitford, salutem. Noveritis me ded. conc. et hac praes. carta conf. Deo etc., omnia de verbo in verbum, sicud in carta terciadecima istius gradus loci primi continentur …

> Roger son of Roger Bertram of Mitford, greetings. Notice that I am giving and in this charter confirming by God, every word in the thirteen charters of yours which are contained in this gradus in locus one … (p34)

It was quite gratifying counting all my little squares back from the thirteenth to the first! Imagine nowadays having a handy paper filing system going back for two hundred years!

---

[48] Fowler, p 27 notes

GRADUS I **De Merlay** Earliest charters Inner area closest to abbey Most undated, but a few before 1265	pages 1-8 Ritton Witton Morpeth to Mitford Morpeth to Hebron Farnley roads in Morpeth	8 – 14 land to north east Ulgham Widdrington Stobswood land to north west Ritton Healeyburn Hesleyhurst land to south Tranwell Riplington Benton	Locus iii 15 - 26 fisheries Benton River Tyne land to south several charters involving mills Shilvington Stannington Eshott	land to the south Mitford Duddo Plessey Clifton Sharplaw Tranwell Hepscott Shadfen Shotton Plessey
GRADUS II **Bertrams of Mitford** Earliest charters close to abbey Most undated but from about 1172 – 1271 incl five from 1307 - 1315	Locus iv 26-32 land between Mitford & Morpeth Meredene Heighley Horton Espley	Locus v 32-39 Horton Shotton Berwick (nr Horton)	Locus vi 39-41 land between Mitford & Morpeth Heighley Benridge Espley 42-45 ecclesiastical charters	south of the Tyne 45-53 CHOPWELL Rivers Tyne and Derwent land exchanged Wolsingham for saltworks at Blyth Locus vij Blyth and Cambois 53-57 two dated 1236 and 1250 STANNINGTON 57-62
GRADUS III **de Umfravill** other families incl Swinburn Gunnerton Balliol one dated 1181 six dated in 1200s one dated 1334	FILTON 62-68 Filton Tolland Kidland Sweethope Carrycoats Swinburn 68-73	KIDLAND 73-83 Coquetdale Alwinton Cheviot moors HUDSPETH 83–95 LYTHEDUN	MORPETH 95-106 grants of land, sales and rent by townspeople	ALDWORTH 107-117 mixed set of charters Higham
GRADUS IIII **Cospatric** earliest probably from late 1100s other families incl Greystokes Flotterton Butiler	CAISTRON 117-148 many land grants incl hermits Greystokes p144 FLOTTERTON 148- 153 BUTILER 154-156	SHARPERTON THIRNUM (FARNHAM) Locus vii 156-159 BICKERTON 160-164 mainly grants about rights of way BIDDLESTONE 164-165 Feritate family	YDINGTON 165 – 179 Locus viii many grants for Infirmary of Seculars	
GRADUS V Walter de Bolam and others many between 1424 and 1489	NEWTON 179-186 Locus i land around Bolam, incl. Newton Grange	ECHEWYK (EASTWICK?) 186-197 1386 to 1489 incls one in English conveying salt pans		
GRADUS VI many between 1416 and 1487	STRETTON Locus i 197-210 Warkworth Stretton Edlingham Buston	SALTWORKS OF WARKWORTH 211-220 many ecclesiastical charters FORUM 220-221 PENDEMORE 221-226 incl Bertram of Bothal	TRITLINGTON 226-238 EARSDON incl many grants for lights at tomb of St Robert	NEWCASTLE, BOOTHS 238- 243 includes leases for booths at Newcastle market, grants for hosts and wine for mass
LOCUS vii GRADUS VI	NEWBIGGIN 244- 247 grants for land and boats	EXTERIOR KNAPELAW 248-255 agreements about St Leonard's and St Cuthbert's chapels SHOTTON & PLESSEY 256-257 agreement re chapels 1491	MERESFEN 257-259 grant of land and tenements with windmill dated 1485 LONGWITTON 259-262 mixed grants 1340-1425	WALLINGTON 262-263 incl perambulation of Rothley and affidavit in English 1487INDEX index of page numbers in original cartulary

The charters were probably arranged in a pigeonhole system. Each *gradus* would be a shelf, and each *locus* a place on the shelf. The arrangement by donor families and geographical places is fairly clear. Places named in lower and upper case, as well as the page numbers, follow the system in the Surtees Society's transcription of the cartulary. Most significant places from the cartulary are included.   Sometimes the charters had topics as their subject, for example those referring to lights for St Robert. Modern spellings are used wherever known.

In the pigeon-hole system we can see how the *gradus* were linked to certain landowners, Gradus I being with the de Merlays, Gradus II with the Bertrams of Mitford, Gradus III with the de Umfravills of Redesdale and Gradus IIII with the Cospatrics. There was an assortment of other donors in other *loci*. Morpeth's charters, which were mainly with local burgesses, were tucked into Gradus III; and those from the Blyth and Cambois area into *locus vij* in Gradus II.

By naming all these donors, and their families past and future, the cartulary brings those people back to life. It shows the links between them and their lands, and we can sense both their piety and their motivation towards the abbey. Wives are often named along with the men, and ancestors and descendants frequently. Although it is at first glance a dry document, through it we can get a picture of medieval life in the fields and hills of Northumberland. These were real people who did real things in this landscape.

Once I'd organised the pigeonhole diagram, I then put all the significant places named in the charters on a map. It was rivetting to see the extraordinary area of land they covered. Our monks were busy people. From the centre point of the abbey next to Morpeth, the lands which they managed range in a clear north west to south east alignment. There were outliers to the north around Warkworth and south towards Newcastle; and one into County Durham. Although Newminster is sometimes said by commentators to be one of the smaller monasteries, compared to Fountains or Melrose for example, there must have been strong organisation at the centre to manage such vast acreages.

Not all the places named would have been active all of the time. Arrangements would come and go, and properties would change hands over the course of the abbey's life. But there is no doubt that we are talking of a substantial operation, lasting for four hundred years from its original first steps through its gradual expansion until the disturbance of the wars with Scotland after 1296, and its continuation until the dissolution in 1537.

The monks of Newminster managed these extraordinary estates through their vast labour force which consisted of their own lay brothers and the local peasantry. It is not often that the labourers get a personal mention in the cartulary. They were essential to the system, and they worked through a series of outlying farms called *granges*. This was a particularly Cistercian form of management. Newminster had a lot of them.

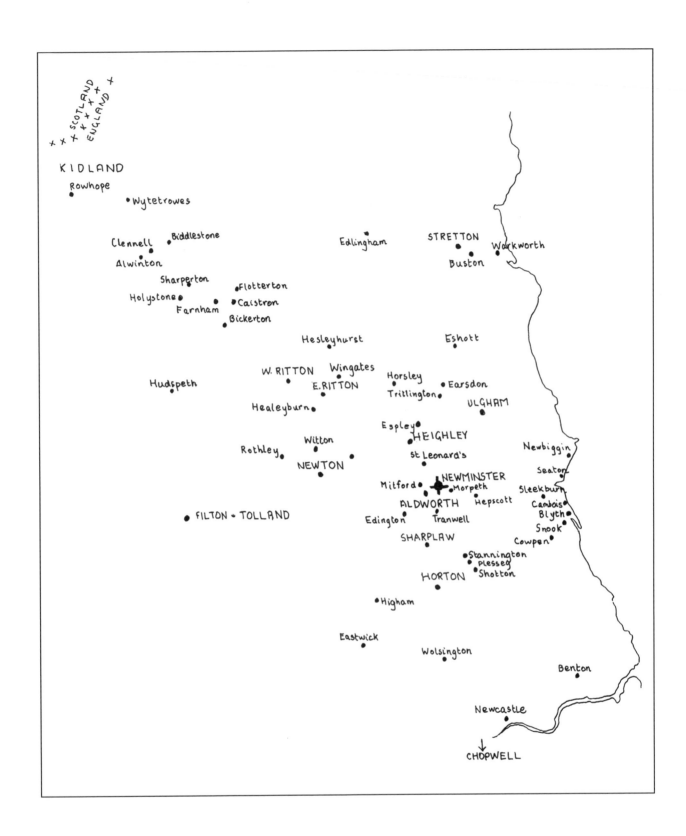

Places where Newminster had significant charters between 1138 and 1493. Granges are marked in capital letters

The granges and the servants

The Cistercians, unlike other monastic orders, were not at first allowed to accept gifts of manors and rectories with the income which they brought. They were to sustain themselves by their own endeavours and the granges were at the heart of this:

> The Cistercians set about assembling the more important of their properties into easily managed units, each to be controlled by a team of lay brethren assigned to the purpose by the monastery, and each to be subject to the general supervision of an official known as the *cellarer*, a member of the religious community and based at the abbey itself. Considered as a store of equipment and produce, the new unit came to be known as a grange, though the word in conventional usage continued to apply to a barn. It was sited, for reasons of control as much practical as moral, within easy reach of the abbey, to which it would return its produce.[49]

We don't know how many lay brothers there were at Newminster and neither do we know how many of the local population helped them. At the Cistercian abbey of Rievaulx, in the time of their most renowned abbot Ailred 1147-1167, there were 140 monks and 500 lay brothers and servants.[50] This figure of 500 did not differentiate between lay brothers and servants; what is certain is that the work of the local populace was essential.

Under the cellarer, the lay brothers would be a reliable source of farm management. Sometimes the human labour force was included as part of the land grants by the donors. The people who lived in the local vills, in little clusters of houses, would be required to labour for the abbey just as they were for any other landowner. As well as working their own strips of land and looking after their own animals, they would be required to take a share of ploughing and harvesting the abbey's fields. They would do this under the supervision of the lay brothers:

> Tied or hired labour on the grange would seem a necessary condition of its working. Certainly the employment of domestic servants may be assumed from the beginning ... but beyond this some allowance at least must be made for the existence of a very much larger force of agricultural labourers, of skilled craftsmen, ploughmen, herdsmen, store-keepers and even dairymaids ... It may be that some of these, with the certain exception of the last, could have been accommodated within the grange court itself ... but it must have been out of the question to do the same for the majority even of the permanent staff, much less for any seasonal additions.[51]

No dairymaids would have been allowed in the male-only precincts of the grange. But although women and girls seldom get a mention in the literature there is no reason to assume that their labour was rejected. Routine milking and cheesemaking was a job in which they were particularly skilled. Out in the fields their work would at least have included haymaking and harvesting.

As for those specifically engaged to work in the granges as servants, we have no details for those of Newminster and can only guess that it was similar to other places. A list of servants at a Benedictine grange in Kent in 1290 consisted of eight ploughmen, a shepherd, a swineherd, an oxherd, a cowherd, a goatherd and a dairymaid. At one of Beaulieu Abbey's important granges in Berkshire there were eight ploughmen, two carters, a hayward, a forester, a baker, a cheese-maker, a porter and a swineherd. In the summer, a cook and his boy, a tithe collector, a cowherd and three shepherds were added.[52]

If we look at our map, we can see where Newminster's granges were. Ulgham and Ritton appeared in the foundation charter of 1138. They are approximately six miles and ten miles from the abbey, journeys which were manageable within a day.

---

[49] Colin Platt, The Monastic Grange in Medieval England, Fordham University Press, 1969, p 12
[50] Platt, p 12
[51] Platt, p 87
[52] Platt, pp 79 – 80.

We can also see Heighley, Horton, Sharplaw, Stretton, Wreighill and Newton granges on the map. Aldworth grange was in the now lost village between Mitford and Morpeth. There were others which are not mentioned in the cartulary but which we know about from different sources. Nunnykirk is not mentioned until the dissolution documents and thus is not shown on this map. Rowhope Grange is in the upper Coquet valley beyond Alwinton and we'll learn more about it later.[53]

Although most of them were within a ten mile radius from the abbey, a few were a lot further away. These include Stretton near Warkworth at about 15 miles, Wreighill at 23 miles, and Rowhope at 35 miles.

We may remember also that ARS Ltd's 2011 survey identified a likely home grange right next to the monastery precinct itself.

There are no known buildings or significant remains of the original granges of Newminster in Northumberland as far as I am aware.

What we do have, though, is a handful of modern place names such as Ulgham Grange and Horton Grange. Anyone who has been to Horton Grange hotel, near Blagdon, will be hard pressed to see any buildings that might make them think of a medieval abbey, even at the nearby site of Old Horton. The same applies to Ulgham Grange, East Sleekburn Grange or Hartburn Grange (called Newton Grange in the cartulary. Hodgson explains it is Hartburn, in his *History of Morpeth*, p 50). We need to bear in mind though that some of the place names we can find on Northumberland maps relate to other abbeys, such as Shilbottle Grange near Alnwick or Anick Grange near Hexham. Sometimes also a much later Victorian or modern house or estate might be given the name *grange* for prestige.

The ordinary people of Northumberland were labouring on these farms while the choir monks were cloistered inside. Whole stretches of countryside as revealed in the charters, from the hills of the Cheviots to the North Sea coast, were being worked for the abbey. It was an important part of medieval life locally; a vast enterprise. Newminster was a great landholder in Northumberland, absorbing the lives of hundreds of people.

The charters
There are over 600 charters in the cartulary and it is impossible in a book like this to discuss more than a few. Once I'd sorted out the pigeonhole diagram and the map, I then had to choose which charters upon which to focus. It was important to look at the heartland properties around Morpeth and Mitford donated by the local barons. The townspeople of Morpeth have their own section. I also chose the south easterly charters of the salt works at Cambois and Blyth. Finally, I would follow the charters from the abbey north westerly to the Cheviots, which has its own chapter later on.

Once I'd chosen my special areas, down went my head to look at the Latin. I focussed on personal names of the donor families; on descriptions of places which would help interpret the landscape; and on colourful details about animals and the movement of people. I've left in my Latin selections, and for those who are interested it shows how much of the language we have inherited when we speak English today. I had a small budget for expert translations.

The pigeonhole diagram above gives page numbers in the cartulary as an aid for those who would like to look at other places. In the following extracts the page number at the end refers to that in the Surtees Society transcription.

---

[53] Ian Roberts, Richard Carlton and Alan Rushworth, Drove Roads of Northumberland, The History Press, 2010, p 40

de Merlay charters

Most of the first charters in Gradus I are from Morpeth's de Merlay family. Directly following the foundation charter of Ranulph and Juliana comes one which confirms which land belongs to the abbey at its heartland in Morpeth. This one is from Ranulph's son, Roger de Merlay I, and the only thing we can say about its date is that it was before the year of his death in 1188:

> … totam vallem inter Morpath et Mitford … ex una parte aquae a recta divisa inter Morpath et Hebre, sicud currit rivulus qui vocatur Fulbeke, et cadit in Cottingburna …

> … all the valley between Morpeth and Mitford … from one side of the water boundary between Morpeth and Hebron, as the river which is called Fulbeck runs, and falls into the Cottingburn … (p2)

He confirms the use of common pasture which is the right of the monks to graze their animals on the commons:

> … apud Witton et apud Morpath et apud Hulgam cum hominibus suis, et homines ejus cum monachis ad eandem pasturam liberum exitum peculiae suae …

> … as far as Witton and as far as Morpeth and as far as Ulgham with their men, and with the monks to these pastures free movement as they need … (p2)

And at Ulgham, one of the earliest granges:

> Et apud Hulgam ad construendas grangias suas dedit eis a nido aquilae, usque ad fontem Egardi, et sicud currit rivulus ejusdem fontis in Linam … ad divisam de Lyntuna…

> And near Ulgham the building of the grange given to them to the nest of the eagle, until the fountain of Edgar, and as the river runs from the fountain into the Lyne … to the boundary of Linton … (p2)

Confirmations of the earliest charters follow from Roger de Merlay II and Roger de Merlay III, including a new mention of a mill at Fulrez. There are two new land donations at Farnley, which I can't place although the same charter mentions Cottingwood and, according to Fowler's notes, a quarry at Blindwell:

> … inter boscum de Cottingwode et aquam de Wanspike, scilicet, apud Blindwell sicud clauditur fossato ab habendum ibi lapidicium …

> … between the wood of Cottingwood and the water of Wansbeck, namely, as far as Blindwell where there is a walled bank to the quarry … (p5)

Roger de Merlay III mentions the sheepfold in one of his charters, on the land near Meredenflat which is between Morpeth and Mitford. This must be an important sheep rearing centre as the same sheepfold is mentioned in a charter from the Bertrams of Mitford which we'll come across a little later:

> … culturam meam, quae vocatur Meredenflat, in territorio de Morpath, juxta berchariam eorundem monachorum …

> … my cultivated land, that is called Meredenflat, in the land of Morpeth, next to the sheepfold of the monks … (p6)

Roger de Merlay III was building his new town in Morpeth after 1239.[54] There are grants for roads, one of which is to the quarry of Holburne which is probably Howburn in the present Bluebell Woods. A note in the cartulary's margin here calls this road Copper Chare:

---

[54] Bridget Gubbins, The Curious Yards and Alleyways of Morpeth, GMDT, 2011, pp 25 - 29

... j viam habentem in latitudine xxxvj pedes, quae extendit del Neugate villae de Morpath versus orientem ... ad antiquam viam, et inde sufficientam viam usque ad quadrariam de Holburne, carris et carrectis, summagiis et hominibus sine impedimento mie vel heredum vel hominum meorum.

... one road having width of 36 feet, extending from Newgate in the town of Morpeth towards the east ... to the old road, and going to the quarry of Holburne, carts and carriages, horseloads and men, without any impediments from my heirs and my men. (pp5-6)

Another charter confirms the free road of Greengate, the location of which we can only guess. It is interesting in that it actually mentions Roger's new town :

... quod cum praedicessores mei concesserint monachis Nov. Mon. libere viam de Grauenegate

... which my predecessors conceded to the monks of Newminster the free road of Greengate.

and

... ad capud aquilonale novae villae de Morpath quam fundavi usque ad crucem lapideam ...

... to the north of the new town of Morpeth which I founded as far as the stone cross ... (p6)

There is a clue as to a main route between Newminster and Newcastle. The same Roger de Merlay III allows the building of a bridge at Horton, about five miles south of Newminster. We'll soon see that the Bertrams of Mitford awarded a grange at Horton so this route, and the movement of traffic along it, is of great importance to the abbey:

Concessi eciam eis firmare pontem de Horton super terram meam ex boriali parte aquae de Blithe, et reparare quociens opus fuerit, et liberam viam et sufficientem summagiis et cariagiis suis versus abbathiam quamdiu terra mea durat. (p4)

I concede also the revenue from the bridge of Horton on my land to the north side of the river Blyth, and to repair it as required, and free way of his horse loads and carriages towards the abbey as long as the land is mine. (p4)

The almost historically-invisible peasantry get a mention in one of Roger de Merlay III's charters in which he grants some extra land at Witton:

Quinque acras terrae arabilis ... que abuttat super crofta husbandorum in territorio de Witton .. et super viam quae ducit versus Wyndegates ad capud boriale ...

Five acres of arable land ... that abuts the croft of the husbandman in the area of Witton ... and over the road which leads towards Wingates to the north ... (p7)

Gradus I also covers charters concerning land some miles south of the abbey. Of particular interest are two grants for fisheries on the Tyne river. In the following example, we can see the typical wording in the charters where the grants require the monks to pray for the souls of the donor and list members of the family in the past and the future. The *pitancias* or pittances do not as in our modern sense mean a tiny morsel but are special gifts of food, in this case perhaps fish for the monks. They are to be served on the anniversaries of those of his family whom he has mentioned:

Rogerus de Merlay, salutem ... me. ded. conc. et hac praes. carta mea conf. ... pro salute animae meae et pro animabus patris et matris mie, et Adae uxoris mei, et Ranulphi filii mei, et omnium antecessorum meorum et heredum, piscarias meas de Benton in Tyna, scilicet, Hames yhare et Burnemuth yare ad faciendum pitancias praedictis monachis ...

Greetings from Roger de Merlay ... I give, concede and with this my charter confirm ... for the health of my soul and those of my father and mother, and Ada my wife and Ranulph my son, and all my ancestors and heirs, my fisheries in Benton on Tyne, namely, Hames and Burnmouth to provide pittances for the said monks ... (p15)

Another important set of charters in this *gradus* are those which Fowler calls *obits* in his marginal notes. Many of them concern donations from the profits of mills, mainly watermills, although one has a rare mention of a windmill at Newham. These *obits* are for prayers to be made on specific days annually for the souls of the named persons. Here are two extracts:

> Ego Richard Gubiun ad peticionem domini Willelmi de Melay avunculi mei … et pro salute animae avae meae dominae Aliciae de Stutebil et matris meae Agnetis de Merlay … redditum xx solidorum percipiendum annuatim … x s. ad Pentecosten, et x s. ad festum Sancti Martini. Et hos xx. assignavi praedictis monachis in molendino meo de Schiluignton …

> I Richard Gubiun at the petition of lord William de Merlay my uncle … and for the benefit of the souls of my Lady Alice of Stuteville and my mother Agnes de Merlay … render 20 shillings annually … 10 shillings at Pentecost, and ten shillings at the feast of Saint Martin. And this twenty shillings I am assigning to the monks from my mill at Shilvington … (pp15-16)

Roger Maudut granted an income from his mill at Eshott:

> … redditum xx s. per annum in molendino meo de Eschette … ij terminus in anno, scilicet, x s. ad festum Sancti Martini in hyeme et x s. ad Pentecosten, ad inveniend. tres pitancias honestas et competentes annuatim … in die Nativitatis Beatae Mariae de x s. secundam vero de v s. in die Sancti Lamberti …

> …rendering 20 shillings annually from my mill at Eshott … twice yearly, namely, 10 shillings at the feast of Saint Martin and 10 shillings at Pentecost, and three good meals annually … on the birthday of Blessed Mary for 10 shillings and the second for five shillings on the day of Saint Lambert … (p17)

Among this long document is a mention of the deserving poor:

> … quicquid remanserit in praedictus tribus diebus detur portario ad portam, ut fideliter pauperibus distribuat pro animabus nostris.

> … anything that remains may be given by the porter at the gate, to the faithful poor distributed for our souls. (p17)

Compassion for the poor indeed; but they were only to have the left-overs!

Bertrams of Mitford charters
The Bertrams lived in their castle on its mound a little further upriver from Morpeth. They were the immediate neighbours of the de Merlays and some historians affirm that Alice, the wife of the first baron William Bertram, was a daughter of William de Merlay.[55] Alice's name is also sometimes spelled Hawys.

William and Alice Bertram founded their own abbey at Brinkburn on the Coquet during the reign of Henry I and therefore before his death in 1135.[56] There must have been many neighbourly conversations, *en francais*, and perhaps rivalry between the two families. We can picture the discussions at the table over the roasted venison and the wine. There would be riding out too and meetings in the watery pastures beside the Wansbeck, as they discussed the boundaries between their baronages and how the water from the river could be made available for the new abbey next to Morpeth.

The contribution of the Bertrams was essential to the foundation of Newminster. Their own abbey at Brinkburn was over the hills in the next valley to the north, a distance of about 10 miles, and which required the fording of two rivers to get there. Despite this, they were very generous to Newminster. As they controlled part of the valley of the Wansbeck river between Mitford and Morpeth, agreements to allow the water to be channelled to the abbey were fundamental. Although it is difficult to date the early charters in this section of Gradus

---

[55] Percy Hedley, Northumberland Families, Vol 1, Society of Antiquaries Newcastle upon Tyne, 1968, p 27
[56] William Page, introduction to Brinkburn Cartulary, Surtees Society Vol 1, 1892

II, we may make a reasonable guess that the first of them would be around the same time as the foundation charter of 1138. It is likely that the abbot of Fountains would only endorse the new abbey at Newminster if the essential water supply from the Wansbeck was secured.

William Bertram, the first baron of Mitford, would have made the earliest donations. We have no exact dates but his son the first Roger was active as baron in 1149.[57] Thus it is quite reasonable that William made donations to the monks as early as 1138.

There is one charter which is out of chronological order in the cartulary, and it takes us right back to him and his son Roger:

> Sciant omnes quod nos Willelmus Bertram et Rogerus Bertram heres meus concessimus et dedimus in perpetuam elemosinam abbathiae S. M. Nov Mon. partem terra de Milford, scil. ex una parte aquae a recta divisa inter me et Ranulfum de Morpath, Meredena, terram quae vocatur Holm …

> Be it known to all that we William Bertram and Roger Bertram my heir concede and give for ever and ever to the abbey of the Blessed Mary of Newminster part of the land of Mitford, namely, from one side of the water to the division between me and Ranulph of Morpeth, Meredene, land which is called Holm … (p39)

Here William Bertram and Ranulph de Merlay, the founder of the abbey, are working out the boundaries of their donations in the Wansbeck valley between Morpeth and Mitford. The name Meredene turns up several times in the early charters. The *mere* part of the name can mean *boundary*.[58]

Roger Bertram, William's son, married Ada. She was the daughter of Hugh de Moreville, the constable of David, king of Scotland.[59] He founded Dryburgh abbey, near Melrose, in the Scottish borders in 1150. All these families took pride in founding monasteries, it seems. Through her there would have been close links with Scotland. The first grant in Gradus II is from Roger and Ada for the water supply.

> Concessi Ab. et monachis Novi Monasterii, terram ad faciendam fossatum suum, et aquam de Wenspik ad Grumbwell, scilicet, ad adducendam ad molendinum suum, pro animabus patris et matris meae, et omnium parentum et antecessorum meorum, in perpetuum elemosinam. (p26)

> I grant to the abbot and the monks of Newminster, land to make a ditch, and water from the Wansbeck to Grumbwell, namely, leading to their mill, for the souls of my father and my mother and all my kin and my ancestors, in perpetual alms. (p26)

This charter is followed by another from Roger:

> Licenciam faciendi et firmandi stagnum suum inter abbathiam et Mitford, super terram meam de Hamestal, et reparandi quando necesso habuerint, et conducendi aquam per stagnum suum ad fossatum suum et per fossatum ad abbathiam.

> We grant a licence to make a millpond between the abbey and Mitford, on my land of Hamestal, repairing it when necessary, and leading the water from the millpond through the ditch to the abbey. (p29)

Whether the word *fossatum,* which is translated as *ditch* here, means it was an unlined and earthen ditch we can't say. It would have taken a considerable time and effort to build a stone-lined channel at least a half mile to the abbey.

---

[57] Hedley, p 27
[58] Allen Mawer, Cambridge University Press, 1920, p 236
[59] Hedley, p 27

The next charter of Roger Bertram I grants some more land by the Wansbeck. This one is particularly interesting because it names a person from the seldom-seen lower levels of society:

> … totam illam placiam, quae est juxta siketam quae descendit in Wanspike juxta terram cultam de Alriesdelf versus orientem, usque ad divisas dictorum monachorum. (p 29)

> … all the land that is next to the valley that comes down to the Wansbeck next to land cultivated by Alriesdelf toward the east, as far as the boundary of the monks.

One of the pigeon holes in Gradus II is *locus vi* and it contains the charters about Horton Grange. Roger Bertram I and his wife Ada confirmed a grant here. Roger's father William had been the first to grant it:

> Rogerus Bertram, salutem. Notum sit vobis ad quorum noticiam literae istae pervenerint vel audienciam, me, peticione ac voluntate Adae uxoris meae et heredum meorum, et consilio fratrum et hominum meorum, dedisse ac conc. et hac. p. c. conf. Deo et monachis Nov Mon., … Hortune cum omnibus suis pertinenciis, scilicet, in pascuis, pratis et pasturis, aquis, molendinis, in stagnis, piscariis et in omnibus aliis asiamentis, et communem pasturam, sicud homines mei de eadem villa ante habuerunt.

> Roger Bertram, greetings. Be it known to you to whose notice or hearing this letter comes, that I with the request and will of my wife Ada and heirs, and the advice of my brother and my men, to have given, conceded and confirmed to God and the monks of Newminster, … Horton, with all its belongings, namely, in pasture, meadow and grazing land, waters, mills, ponds, fisheries and all other provisions, and common pasture, just as my men who lived in this village held previously. (p32)

Many of the charters when granting land use the phrase *cum omnibus suis pertinenciis,* which means *with all its appurtenances* or *belongings*. In this case it looks as though the men who lived in the village were given as part of the grant of Horton to the abbey; that they were not thrown off, but would now have to serve other masters.

We do hear of abbeys which threw people off the land, Rievaulx in Yorkshire being an often-quoted example. However as the monks required work to be done on such land, as we saw in the extract from Platt earlier, it seems reasonable to assume that they often stayed where they were.

This charter also describes a perambulation by Hugh the dapifer, Roger Bertram's steward, and others:

> Hanc donacionem hujus villae feci eis per suas divisas, sicud Hugo dapifer meus et alli hominess mei perambulaverunt, sicud divisa ejusdem Horton et Scotton ascendit de Blida, et vadit at petariam ad fossatum, et per fossatum ad cestras …

> This donation of this vill was made along its boundaries, which Hugh my dapifer and others of my men have perambulated, as the boundary between Horton and Shotton went up to the Blyth river, and came to the peat diggings by the ditch, and by the ditch to the camps … (p32)[60]

The rent the monks have to pay is clearly shown:

> … viginti marcas et Willelmo heredi meo unum catur' precii xx s., et exinde reddent mihi et heridibus meis annuatim x libr. at Pentecosten …

> … twenty marks and to William my heir one hunting horse (or hound) at a value of twenty shillings, and paying to me and my heirs ten pounds at Pentecost … (p33)

---

[60] *dapifer:* one who brings meat to table; hence the official title of the steward of a king's or nobleman's household. OED

The translation of *catur'* is uncertain according to Fowler. At the bottom of the page in the cartulary, he notes that it could be either horse or hound.

Among the charters in Gradus II, *locus vi* we find many about Heighley, the area which is now well-known locally because of Heighley Gate garden centre. The word is spelled in a variety of ways throughout the charters.

Roger Bertram I's first charter for Heighley grants the vill itself and all its belongings.

> ... villam quae dicitur Heithlau et quicquid ad illam pertinet, per suas rectas divisas sicud eis coram meis hominibus demonstravi ... Insuper concessi eis communem pasturam terra meae in bosco et in plano, praetor Widinglei et Benrigden ultra divisam quam eis demonstravi, moram apud Hespeley ad focalia sua.

> ... the village that is called Heighley and whatever pertains to it, from the boundaries that they have demonstrated in the presence of my men ... as well I grant to the same common pasture on my land in woodlands and fields, beyond Widinglei and Benridge beside the boundaries that they demonstrated, the moor as far as Espley for their fuel. (p39–40)

The monks had to pay rent which was to be seven marks annually, payable on the feast of Saint Martin. Roger also stipulated that he and his wife were to receive the prayers of the monks and that they would be buried in the abbey.

Roger Bertram I died in 1177. His son William inherited the barony. There are very few charters from his period between 1177 and approximately 1199.[61] However he did release the monks from paying their seven marks' rent for Heighley:

> Remisisse et quietam clamasse ... sextam marcam de firma de Heithlau, quam dederunt patri meo et mihi.

> I remit and quitclaim six marks of revenue from Heighley that they have given to my father and me. (p40)

Quitclaim means the release of financial or any other burdens.

Another of William's few charters is very important because it confirms the donation of Horton and Heighley granges, taking them back beyond his father Roger to his grandfather William, to the earliest days of the foundation of Newminster:

> Willelmus Bertram, salutem ... confirmaciones ac libertates quas pater meus et avus meus eis dederunt et cartis suis confimaverunt, scilicet, Heithlau cum omnibus pertinenciis suis ... et Horton cum omnibus pertinenciis suis, et illam partem petariae quam ibi habent.

> William Bertram, greetings ... confirmation and freedoms that my father and grandfather have given to them and by their charters have confirmed, namely, Heighley with all its belongings ... and Horton with all its appurtenances, and the part of the turbary which they have in that place. (p34)

We will remember that Roger and Juliana de Merlay granted the granges of Ulgham and Ritton, the former to the east and the latter to the west of the abbey beside Morpeth, in the foundation charter of 1138. So now we have learned that at an early date granges were also granted by the Bertrams to Newminster just to the north of the abbey at Heighley; and one was to the south at Horton. The land all around the abbey was clearly well under its control from its beginnings.

After William came his son Roger Bertram II. He was baron from about 1199 to 1242.[62] His one significant charter in the cartulary is a confirmation of the grants of his ancestors. From

---

[61] Hedley, p 28

this there is further supporting evidence that both Horton and Heighley were granted originally by the first William Bertram as early as the 1130s:

> ex dono Willelmi Bertram, proavi mei ... terram inter abbathiam et Mitford ... Heithlau per suas rectas divisas ... et cum omn. pertinenciis suis quam habent ex dono Rogeri Bertram avi mei ... et praes. carta conf. Hortone per suas rectas divisas ...

> from the gift of my great-grandfather William Bertram ... land between the abbey and Mitford ... Heighley along its straight boundaries ... and with all the appurtenances that they have from the gift of that they were gifted by Roger Bertram my grandfather ... and the charter confirms Horton along its straight boundaries ... (p30)

Roger Bertram II's son is also called Roger. Confusingly, in the charters he is known as Roger son of Roger, which means Roger III. Don't worry if you are completely befuddled. I was too! The details can be worked out from the Bertram family tree in the appendix to this book.

This Roger III has a long and detailed charter in Gradus II which is full of local topographical details. His baronage was from about 1258 to 1271 and in this he is confirming the charters of his antecedents:

> ... partem terrae meae in territorio de Mitford ... a Meredene quae est divisa inter baronias de Mitford et Morpeth, terra quae vocatur Holm ...

> ... part of my land in Mitford ... from Meredene which is the boundary between the baronies of Mitford and Morpeth, in land that is called Holm ... (p27)

Detailed descriptions follow of the boundaries including mention of a *bercaria,* a sheep fold:

> ... et sic sequendo semitam illam versus orientem usque in praenominatam Meredene, ex occidentali parte bercariae dictorum monachorum ...

> ... and following the lane towards the east as far as the aforesaid Meredene, from the western side of the sheepfold of the said monks ... (p27)

He is reserving the rights of the chase for his family:

> Salva michi et heredibus meis de corpore meo euntibus, tantum chacia in eadem terra ad bestias silvestris ...

> Saving for myself and my heirs of my body all the hunting in this land for the beasts of the forest ... (p27)

He releases the monks from a former payment of bread and other food in Lent that his antecedents had received from them:

> ... et per cartam meam quiet. clamasse pro me et heredibus meis dictis monachis et eorum successoribus in perpetuum panem et pulmentum ...

> .., and through this charter, I quitclaim by me and my heirs to the aforesaid monks and their successors in perpetuity bread and food ... (p27)

In this same charter, the monks may build a sluice gate across the ditch;

> ... et licebit eisdem monachis eandem terram claudere fossato et idem fossatum renovare et reparere ...

---

[62] Hedley, p 28

... and I license the same monks the same land to build a sluice gate across the ditch and to renovate and repair the same ditch ... (p27)

Roger Bertram III also licences the monks to quarry stone at a place called Tamdene:

> ... licenciam capiendi lapides de quadraria de Tamdene, et cariandi libere per terram meam quantumcumque et quandocumque voluerint ...

> ... we licence the quarrying of stone from the quarry of Tamdene, and free carriage through my territory as much as and whenever they want ... (p30)

There is a long confirmation charter by Roger Bertram III dated Easter, 28 March 1250, during the reign of Henry III (1216-1272). It seems to summarise just about all the grants made by himself and his ancestors. After the usual courtesies at the beginning, it lists the many donations his family has made:

> Noveritis me ded. conc. et hac praes. carta mea conf. ... maneriis, boscis, pastures, viis et semitis, pratis, molendinis, petariis, bercariis, aquis, stagnis, piscariis et in omnibus aliis locis quaecumque habent ex donis vel comfirmacionibus aliqujus antecessorum meorum.

> Notice that I have given, granted and confirmed in this my charter ... manors, woods, pastures, roads and paths, meadows, mills, turbaries, sheepfolds, waters, ponds, fisheries and in all the places which they have from the gifts or confirmations of my ancestors. (p31)

This is followed with many details again of Horton and Heighley granges, the land and waters between Mitford and the abbey, and more. At the end, he confirms a relaxation of the annual rent of twenty marks for the granges. Perhaps the abbot had been putting pressure on him. It sounds like there was a big festive gathering at this event. It is witnessed by a list of ten of the local gentry:

Robert of Cresswell
Robert of Cambo
Hugo of Bolbec
Roger de Merlay
J. de Halton
William Bokeley
John of Plessey
John of Eslington
Roger Bertram of Bothal
Adam Barett.

Suddenly, there is a brief charter on page 34 in which Roger Bertram III confirms the previous thirteen which were mentioned earlier. It is at the end of a section within *locus vi*.

> ... et hac praes. carta. conf. Deo etc., omnia de verbo in verbum, sicud in carta terciadecima istius gradus loci primi continetur.

> ... and this charter confirms in God ... word for word ... all the charters in the thirteen of this *gradus* which the first *loci* contain. (p34)

Despite the just-described charter of Easter 1250, when Roger Bertram III listed in great detail all the previous charters in front of ten witnesses and reduced the payments, it seems that the abbot was not contented.

I can imagine him asking the monk in charge of the charters to request another favour of Bertram.

"*Mon frere*, would you please see if you can persuade his lordship to write a simple confirmation of all the previous charters. It would make life so easy."

And Roger kindly obliged. The organisation was good, and the record has survived to impress us.

This set of charters from the Bertrams has allowed us to picture the lanes and highways from the abbey out into the countryside. To the north, up the slopes of the Wansbeck river, the lay brothers would manage the grange at Heighley and supervise the labourers cutting turf at Espley. Through the land that is now Lancaster Park housing estate and past Fairmoor they would trundle with their wagons and guide the flocks. It is not possible now to trace the routeways. They have been altered over the centuries beyond recognition.

The way south is different. There is still a clear road between Newminster Abbey and Horton, passing through Tranwell hamlet and Duddo. Along here the shepherds will have guided their flocks and the carters driven the oxcarts for the turf, year after year. Nowadays this route is a back road between Morpeth and Tyneside, popular with cyclists. They have to cross with care the narrow hump-backed bridge over the Blyth river at Bellasis which could well be on the same site as the earlier bridge granted to the abbey by Roger de Merlay III.

Morpeth townspeople's charters

Alver the butcher, Thomas the son of Alot, Lambert and Matilda his wife, Richard the mason, Alvery the mason and Johanna his wife, Richard the carpenter, Henry of Thornton the clerk, Richard Goule the smith, Adam the forester and Alice his wife, William the currier, Richard Graffard and Agnes his wife, Robert de la Lawe, William the dyer: all these Morpeth people can be found in the cartulary.

They have a special *locus* in Gradus III. These are the burgesses, or townspeople, as distinct from the great landowners and it makes a refreshing change to think about them after the grandeur of the barons and their families. They too had an interest in donating charitably to the abbey. Many of them donated rent from their properties in Morpeth and the familiar names of Oldgate and Newgate are found. Each property was defined by its place between the neighbouring ones. The charter would state how much was to be paid and on which dates of the year.

Here is an extract from Alver the butcher's donation:

> Aluerius carnifex de Morpath … ded. conc. et h.p.c.m conf. Deo et B. M. abb. et conv. Novi Mon. … unam rodam terrae in villa de Morpath, quae quidem jacet in antiqua via inter terram Rogeri Pantill et terram Johannis Langer … ad inveniendum per provisionem Prioris praedictae domus Nov. Mon. … die Beati Francisci confessoris … pitanciam competentem. … tenebo vj denarios die Natalis Domini eisdem annuatim persolvendo …

Alver the butcher of Morpeth … I give, concede and in this my charter confirm to God and Blessed Mary the abbot and convent of Newminster … one rood of land in the town of Morpeth, which lies on this ancient road between the land of Roger the Tiler and the land of John Langer … for finding provisions for the Prior of the aforesaid house New Minster … on the day of Blessed Francis the confessor … an adequate pittance … paying six pence on Christmas Day every year … (p96)

Here is one from William the dyer:

Willelmus tinctor de Morpath … conf. abb. et conv. Novi Mon. duos s. annui redditus recipiendos de illis terris et tenementis … inter terras Willelmi sacerdotis de Bedlyntona ex parte orientali et terras Roberti Fullonis ex parte occidentali, quae se extendunt ab alta via usque Cottingburn … ad festa Pentec. et S. Martini in hyeme per aequales porciones …

William the dyer or Morpeth… I confirm to the abbot and convent of Newminster two shillings yearly from the receipts of these lands and tenements … between the land of William the priest of Bedlington on the eastern side and the lands of Robert the fuller on the west side, that extends from the old road as far as Cottingburn … at the feast of Pentecost and Saint Martin in equal portions … (p105)

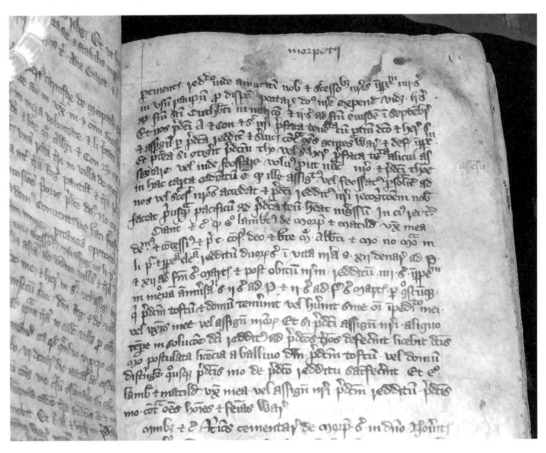

From the Castle Howard Archive.
Reproduced with kind permission of the Hon. Simon Howard

The photograph from the cartulary shows some of the Morpeth section. The town's name appears at the top of the page.

It contains a lease from the abbey to a local man:

… Thomae filio Alot de Morpeth j messuagium et ij rodas terrae cum pertinenciis, quae jacent inter terram quae fuit quondam Willelmi Palmer ex una parte et terram Johannis Pantill ex altera in le Aldgate in villa de Morpeth. … reddendo in perpetuum iiij s. in usum pauperum pro *disposicione portarii domus nostrae expendi; videlicet, ij.s. ad festum Sancti Cuthberti in Marcio et ij. s. ad festum ejusdem in Septembri.*

... to Thomas son of Alot of Morpeth one messuage and two roods of land with its belongings, that lie between land of William Palmer on the one side and of John Pantill on the other in Oldgate in the village of Morpeth. ... rendering for ever four shillings to be distributed to the poor at the gate of our house; that is two shillings at the feast of Saint Cuthbert in March and two shillings at the same feast in September. (p 96)

Thomas's name can be seen in the middle of the first paragraph in the photograph, six lines down, abbreviated to *Tho.*

Next, Lambert of Morpeth and Matilda his wife set up a regular payment to the abbey. This one can be seen in the photograph:

Sciant, etc. quod ego Lambertus de Morpeth et Matild' uxor mea dedimus et. conc. et p. c. conf. ... redditum duorum solidorum in vita nostra, scilicet xij denar. ad Pentecosten et xij ad festum S. Martini, et post obitum nostrum redditum iiij s. in perpetuum ... (p96)

Notice, etc., that I Lambert of Morpeth and Matilda my wife give and concede and confirm ... a payment of two silver shillings during our lifetime, namely twelve pence at Pentecost and twelve at the feast of St Martin, and after our death a payment of four shillings in perpetuity ...

In the inset second paragraph in the photograph, the words *Lambertus de Morpeth et Maltild uxor mea* can be identified.

This sample, the first we have looked at from the main cartulary, has survived in a much clearer condition than the portions of the *ancient roll* which we've seen so far.

Cambois and Blyth charters

The road to the sea between Newminster and Cambois was a busy one. A group of charters show that two of the essential ingredients of monastic life, coal and salt, were provided in the area of Cambois and Blyth. This is now an industrialised landscape crossed by pylons. The Blyth river is joined here by the Sleekburn and they merge into the tidal estuary. The south side of the Blyth river is now fully urbanised.

The word *snook* means a sharp pointed projection of land.[63] The pointed *snook* between the Blyth and the Sleekburn is farmland and the farm there has the name East Sleekburn Grange. Although no-one living in the cottages there has any such idea, the *grange* name could historically date back to the lands farmed by Newminster Abbey.

---

[63] Stan Beckenstall, Place Names and Field Names of Northumberland, Tempus, 2006, p 69

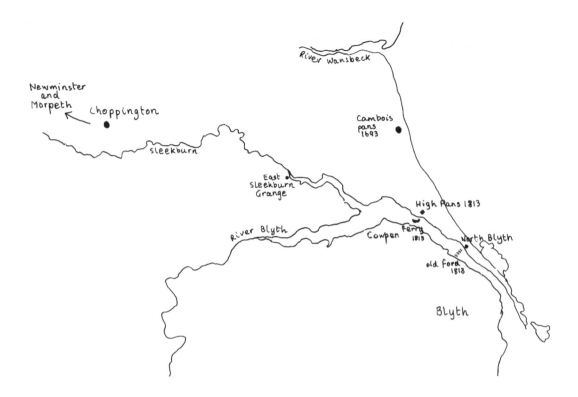

This map is compiled from evidence in two maps dated 1693 and 1813, both of which can be found in A History of Northumberland, Volume 9, pages 348 and 356. They give an idea of where Newminster's saltworks might have been, at High Pans and Cambois. Coal workings took place as well, on both sides of the Blyth river. Dissolution documents of 1537 mention saltworks, coal mining and a granary at *Blythsnok*. The two pointed areas could be the *snooks* mentioned in the charters. (There is a later use of this curious word in the area which is now in Blyth town itself, but this is probably unconnected with the Newminster charters. See Craster, pp 349 – 356.)

This whole area was of great value to the monks. Whereas Newminster's workings were north of the river Blyth, both Brinkburn and Tynemouth Priories' were to the south of the river.[64]

The charters for this area are in Gradus II, following those of Chopwell which is in County Durham. This is logical as far as the monks were concerned as Cambois lies in Bedlingtonshire, to the north of the river Blyth, which was in the control of the Bishop of Durham. Cambois and Blythmouth have their own pigeonhole, *locus* vij, within Gradus II.

The first charter is from Robert of Winchester and Alice his wife.

> Robertus de Wyncestre, salutem. Sciatis quod ego et Alicia uxor mea dedimus et concessimus, consilio et voluntate domini nostril Galfridi episcopi Dunelm., Roberto abb. Nov Mon. salinus nostras super Blitham … cum tofto et crofto … et totam piscacionem aquae de Blitha et Slikeburnmuth … usque ad mare … et communam pasturam averiis suis … et liberum exitum et reditum per totam terram nostram per vias per quas alii homines ambulant … (p53-54)
>
> Robert of Winchester, greetings. Notice that I and Alice my wife have given and conceded with the advice and favour of our bishop Galfred of Durham to Robert the abbot of Newminster our salt works at Blyth … with toft and croft … and all the fishing in the waters of Blyth and

---

[64] H H Craster, A History of Northumberland, Vol 9, 1909, p 223

Sleekburnmouth ... as far as the sea ... and common pasture for their animals ... and free comings and goings through all our land along the roads where everyone moves ...

This was indeed as significant as any foundation charter and would have been negotiated at the earliest establishment of the abbey. Fowler's notes say that Galfrid Rufus was bishop between 1133 and 1140.[65] Salt was an essential ingredient for any enterprise, as the preservation of winter supplies of meat and fish depended on it. Three later bishops confirmed the right to the saltworks in the cartulary and in the third document Bishop Nicholas remitted all payments by the monks. This last can be dated to between 1241 and 1248.[66]

Adam of Cambois must be a significant local man, as he appears in a group of six charters. Here are some extracts:

Ego Adam de Kamhus relaxavi ... quietam clamavi de me et her. meis ... in salinis de Blithemuth ...

Ego Adam de Camhous dedi ... totam terram ... quae jacent in occidentali parte areae salinariae dictorum monachorum ... Dedi pratum quod vocatur le Frereleche ...

Ego Adam de Camhous dedi ... x acras terrae cum pertinenciis, de meo dominico in territorio de Kamhous, cilicet, in cultura que vocatur Medrig ex aquilonali parte salinae de Blithemuthe ... tantum terram in eadem villa.

I Adam of Cambois have released ... and quitclaimed of me and my heirs in the saltworks of Blythmouth ... (p54)

I Adam of Cambois have given ... all the land ... that lies on the west side of the saltworks of the aforesaid monks ... I have given the meadow that is called the Frereleche ... (p55)

I Adam of Cambois have given ... ten acres of land with all its belongings, from my domain in Cambois, demonstrably, in the cultivated land that is called Medrig from the north side of the saltworks of Blythmouth ... thus all the land in this village. (p55)

The fourth one is of fundamental importance in that it also allows the monks to mine or gather coal:

... et totam terram quam habui in illa parte agri, quae vocatur le Snoc ... et praeterea dedi eis pasturam iiij^{or} bobus vel iiij^{or} vaccis in defenso del Snoc ... Et dedi et conc. eisdem monachis ut capiant algam maris ad impinguendam eandem terram, et viam ad libere ducendum eam super praed. terras, et ad carbonem maris capiendum ...

... and all the land that I have in this side in farming, that is called the Snook ... and as well I have given the pasture for four oxen as well as four cows in the enclosure of Snook ... and I have given and conceded to the same monks the gathering of seaweed to improve their land ... and along the road the free movement over these lands, and for the gathering of sea coal ... (p55)

The fifth charter in this section is from three men of Cambois: Adam, Alan and Richard. It is one of the few which is dated, at 1236:

... est concordia facta inter Abb. et Conv. Novi Mon. ex una parte et Adam et Alanum et Ricardum de Kamhus ex altera ... relaxaverunt et quietam clamaverunt ... suis antiquam viam in campo de Kamhus ... inter Slikeburn at Kambus versus salinam de Blithmuth ... et hominibus et averiis suis et summagiis et kariagiis et omnibus aliis rebus suis, magnam viam quae tendit de Chabyngton per moram usque in villam de Kamhus ...

---

[65] Fowler, notes, p 53
[66] Fowler, notes, p 42

> ... this is an agreement between the Abbot and Convent of Newminster on one side with Adam and Alan and Richard of Cambois on the other ... they have released and quitclaimed ... their old road in the fields of Cambois .. between Sleekburn and Cambois towards the saltworks of Blythmouth ... and of their men and beasts and horseloads and carts and all their things, along the great road which leads from Choppington through the moor as far as the village of Cambois ... (p56)

Choppington is a small settlement between Morpeth and Cambois. This enables us to guess something of the route between the two settlements.

The last charter to the abbey in this section concerns Cowpen on the south side of the Blyth river:

> Elias de Kirkeman et Aliz de Caruill uxor ejus, salutem. ... dedimus ... quatuor acras terrae cum pertinenciis in territorio de Coupoun, scilicet, super the Milneflat ij acras terrae, et in le Snok ij acras.

> Elias of Kirkeman and Alice of Caruill his wife, greetings. We give ... four acres of land with appurtenances in the land of Cowpen, namely, above the Millflat two acres of land, and in the Snook two acres. (pp56-57)

This is immediately followed in the cartulary by a *memorandum*, a note written by the monks to themselves. It is dated 1250 and is worth looking at more closely:

> Memorandum quod Abbas et Conventus dimiserunt ad firmam Roberto filio Roberti Copoun iiij acras terrae in territorio de Copoun usque ad terminum xx annorum, pro tribus solidis per annum ... et illam firmam solvat converso de Blithemuth qui fecerit moram ibi. (p57)

> Memorandum that the Abbot and Convent give up to the working of Robert son of Robert of Cowpen four acres of land in the territory of Cowpen for twenty years, for three shillings yearly ... and this rent paid to the lay brother of Blythmouth who works the moor there. (p57)

When he was writing his section of the *The History of Northumberland*, the historian H H Craster understood that Robert was an unfree man, a serf. He confirms the above:

> The four acres were forthwith granted by the abbot and convent on lease to Robert, son of Robert, the serf previously mentioned, to hold at a rent of three shillings, the rent to be received by a lay brother who had management of the abbey salt pans on the north bank of the river.[67]

The serf whom Craster *previously mentioned* is found in a Latin transcript on the previous page of his history. Alina de Bolam was conveying to Elias Kirkeman and his wife Alice various properties and a serf named Robert son of Robert.

> quietum clamaverunt ... predictis Elye et Alicie et heredibus ipsius Alicie totum jus et clamium quod habuerunt in nativitate Roberti filii Roberti de Copum et tocius sequele sue in perpetuum.

> they release claim ... to the aforesaid Elias and Alice and the heirs of Alice herself .... all right and claim which they have had in the birth of Robert son of Robert of Cowpen and all his progeny in perpetuity. [68]

The unfree Robert son of Robert of Cowpen thus had a contract for twenty years, for which he paid rent to the abbey, so he must have been expecting to earn money. He was obviously a worthy candidate to manage four acres and to cross the river with his payment to the lay brother on the other side of the Blyth river. This is a rare find. He is the only person from the lowest ranks of society for whom I have found evidence in the cartulary, albeit indirect, engaged in any kind of financial relationship with Newminster.

---

[67] Craster, p 317
[68] Craster, p 316

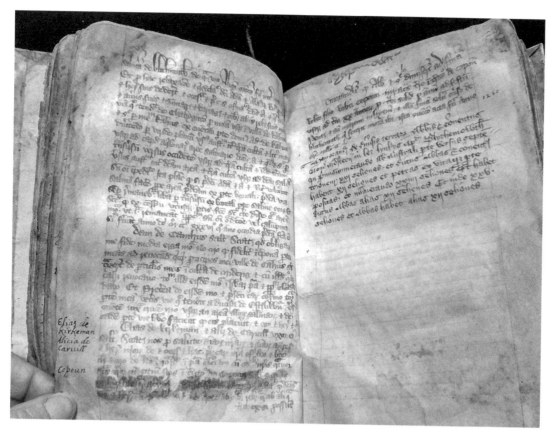

Extract from the cartulary showing the name of Robert the serf of Cowpen

From the Castle Howard Archive. Reproduced with kind permission of the Hon. Simon Howard

In the photograph of these pages from the cartulary, we can see the names of *Elias de Kirkeman* and *Alicia de Caruill* in the left margin, and if we look carefully the serf *Roberto filio Roberti Copoun* is at the beginning of the second line on the page on the right.

The final entry in *locus vii* about Blyth and Cambois is a memorandum listing the number of *selions* which they have in the links of Blythmouth. Selions are strips of ploughed land in an open field system.[69] We cannot be certain about the size of these selions although typically the strips were 220 yards by 22 yards, totalling an acre:

> Memorandum de divisis terrarum Abbatis et Conventus Novi Monasterii in lez Lynkys apud Blythemowth … numerando … versus septentrionem xxj seliones, et dictus abbas et conventus habent xij seliones et petras ex utraque parte positas, et numerando xxiiij seliones, et habet dictus abbas alias xij seliones, et inde xxv seliones, et abbas habet alias xij seliones. (p57)

> Memorandum of the boundaries of land of the Abbot and Convent of Newminster in the links at Blythmouth … numbering … towards the north 21 selions, and the said abbot and convent have 12 selions and peat-workings from the other side, and numbering 24 selions, and the said abbot has another 12 selions, and from that 25 selions, and the abbot has another 12 selions.

This was a significant area of land and the local people would be working on it for the benefit of the abbey.

Thus salt production, coal mining and farming were all taking place in this estuarine landscape, probably with connections at low tide by fords. This landscape, so utterly

---

[69] Mark Bailey, The English Manor, Manchester University Press, 2002, p 246

changed nowadays, was full of people at work. They would be mining and shovelling coal; tending the smoky fires as the salt water was evaporated; raking up white heaps of salt; loading and driving ox-drawn wagons to Morpeth, Brinkburn and Tynemouth. Some would be working on the long and narrow selions, up and down, behind the oxen and others tending the flocks and herds. It is a picture hard to imagine in the post-industrial landscape of today.

Saltmaking at Cambois and Blyth by the Newminster monks

The most likely early method of producing salt at Blyth and Cambois by the monks of Newminster Abbey was called *sleeching*. This was certainly the method used at their Warkworth site, at a place called Gloster Hill, where a large sleeching mound survives in precisely the location indicated by the Newminster cartulary (pp 211-212).

In this method, the salt-impregnated surface silt, or *sleech*, on the upper part of a saltmarsh foreshore was scraped up, and the salt leached out to form a strong brine. This was then boiled in lead pans in a working hut called a *saltcote*, using either peat or wood fuel.

The waste silt was dumped to form large *sleeching mounds* beside the leaching area. Once these were established the saltcotes were often located on top of them to avoid storm-surge flooding. The sleech harvesting had to be undertaken in dry summer weather, and the saltmakers were probably tenants or lay brothers fitting their saltmaking into the agricultural cycle. However if either the sleech or the concentrated brine was stored, the boiling process could be undertaken at other times of the year, allowing the possibility of full-time industrial saltmaking.

By the end of the Middle Ages sleeching was being replaced by the *panhouse* process, in which seawater was raised and fed into very large wrought-iron pans housed in a permanent building. This was boiled using coal fuel. The whole works was often referred to as a *pan* or *saltpan*. Although the fuel consumption per unit of salt was far greater for seawater than for concentrated brine, perhaps nine times as much, the process was much less labour-intensive and took up less space. It was almost independent of the weather and seasons, and it became economic once efficient coalmining and coal-burning methods had been developed to provide cheap and abundant fuel on coastal coalfields. The panhouse process seems to have been perfected on the Firth of Forth in the mid 15th century, possibly by the Cistercians of Newbottle Abbey, and was coming into use in north east England by the end of the century. A reference to *salt pannes* and *colrakes,* or coal rakes, in the Newminster cartulary at Blyth in 1493 shows that the new technology had been adopted by that time.

David Cranstone   March 2014

There is another set of charters which are not assembled as a group in the pigeonhole diagram. They are those in an alignment between Newminster and Kidland in the Cheviot hills, along the pathways of the flocks to the summer pastures. As the lay brothers and the servants led their animals, they would pass through lands for which they needed rights of way; they would encounter other herders; and they would use the monuments of those days to keep track of the paths. This journey, transhumance as we call it now, took place in early summer, the flocks and herds returning when the days grew cooler in early autumn.

These journeys are a fascinating aspect of the story of Newminster, an important part of the system of land management. When I had the idea for this book, I knew that part of it would be to follow the tracks of the herds to the hills. At the back of my mind was something even more challenging. I had the chance to go to a land were people were still making these annual treks, where they are walking up to the hills with their animals along the ancient ways, as their ancestors had done for generations. And thus I would learn what it had been like for the monks, the lay brothers and their servants so many centuries ago in Northumberland.

4   Romanian journey

Packing the cart

"Write it, write it," calls out Florica, as she stuffs plastic sacks with her family's clothes. Old jackets, acrylic jumpers, trousers, scarves, underwear, in they all go. She pulls up some wooden barrels. Cabbages, huge loaves of homemade bread, vinegar, beans, tins of meat, peppers, green beans, biscuits, great bags of flour, yeast, macaroni, food needed for a three month stay in the mountains. Legs of pork which include the hooves, slabs of fat, tubs of home-produced brandy and wine, blankets, great sheepskin coats, saucepans, bread pans, chemical rennet, an iron stove, all are assembled ready.

Florica wants me to list everything. I am sitting on a wooden stool in the vine-shaded courtyard of her village house; ready to find out what I can about transhumance where it still takes place from a Romanian village to the summer pastures in the Carpathian mountains.

It has been some hundreds of years since the shepherds made the annual journeys with the flocks and herds from Newminster up to the Cheviot hills. There is nowhere to find out how they did it, no records, no personal accounts. So I would learn what I could in Romania.

This is to be a 59 kilometre journey to the village's upland pastures at Micau. It is about 36 miles, a similar distance from Newminster to the Cheviots. We will start at about 500 metres and end at over 1600 metres. The journey will be on foot, continuously over 24 hours, and I am 67 years old. I am unsure how well I will cope, but determined to do it. The family comprises Florica, her husband Nicolae, sons Stefu and Lie, daughter Corina and her husband Ioan. They are relaxed about me coming, and re-assure me the pace would be slow. It doesn't seem to occur to them that I will hold them up or cause any problems.

Every year, after the haymaking is completed in June, the journey is made. It has gone on for centuries. For three months, Florica, Nicolae and Stefu will care for the sheep in the mountains while Lie looks after the lowland farm and drives up weekly in the family's tractor to collect the cheese for sale. The sheep make the journey on foot. The cattle are taken by truck half of the way, along the asphalt road as far as it goes, and walk the rest of the way. The tractor pulls the *caruta,* the wooden open wagon, loaded with all the necessaries. Until five years ago the *caruta* was pulled by a horse.

The *traseu,* the journey, is deeply traditional. It is linked with orthodox Christianity and probably much more ancient practices. Going to the summer pastures, where the fresh green growth nourishes the sheep and hence feeds the people, means survival. If the season is good, it might mean accumulating some surplus wealth. It would have had the same importance in the border hills between Northumberland and Scotland.

....

The last milking

On Friday afternoon at about 3 pm, 22nd June 2012, the *caruta* is brought into the yard and everything is loaded. Nicolae gives me a big formal welcome, shaking my hand and talking about God in the mountains. I have only modest Romanian, but I get the gist. He is a shortish man with a tanned intelligent face.

By 5 pm we have moved to the sheep folds.

The ewes are hanging around near the fold. Lie goes to collect them. With a few whistles and without a dog he clusters them all together and brings them into the fold. The ewes are obviously used to this routine. Although they get whacked quite frequently as Lie drives them, they don't seem to be flighty or scared.

A heap of wool is lying on the ground. The sheep have been shorn but the wool is almost worthless. It is the milk which is valued for making cheese.

The 130 ewes are milked for the last time before the journey starts. Corina's three-year old daughter Ioana is in the fold with a little stick, helping to move the ewes towards her uncle and grandparents who are doing the milking. Nicolae, Florica and Stefu sit on stools. The ewes are moved through little gates, one at a time, where they are grabbed by their tails or rear ends. Their two teats are milked by hand through the back legs.

The last milking before the journey starts

The four wolf-like dogs are hanging around, not doing much, but surely sensing that something is going to happen. This is not a normal day.

When the milking is finished the other 170 sheep, consisting of lambs and about ten rams, are brought into the fold. Now all 300 are together. The sheep are panting in discomfort because of the hot weather.

Eight bells on leather straps are brought out. Stefu, Lie and Ioan select strong ewes and grab them, putting on the bells around their necks.

Next, Florica brings out a glass jar which looks like an old pickle bottle with the label still on, full of rather grubby-looking water. With great seriousness, she sprinkles this water across the flock of sheep and recites some words. I remember that a few days ago, on Whit Sunday, I'd observed the priests in a nearby village blessing jars of water that the people had brought. The water was from the villagers' wells. I had only understood a few words of what the priests were saying but remembered *God we pray you … animals … work … land … garden.* I think that in the villages this is an ancient agricultural religion, an appeal to God or the gods who control the fertility of the land and thus the welfare of the people.

Before we leave, the sheep are to be counted. The three young men open the fold gate, and let the animals out one at a time, where they remain in a group. Surprisingly to me, the men announce that there are 300 *precis*, exactly.

The dogs are called. Urs, the youngest, had been fed some bloody meat from an animal newly killed. This may have been to encourage him. The other dogs aren't allowed to have any. Urs doesn't come when called but no-one worries, and he does turn up later. The dogs are semi-independent. They seem to come if they choose to.

The priest blessed the villagers' jars of water

A young mare called Luci is with us. Like the dogs, she is not restrained in any way.

Now I begin to see how the flocks are moved. Corina goes ahead. She calls the sheep and they follow her in a wide line. She is young, slim and efficient, and calls them with assurance. We are leaving the lowland *pasuna*, the village's common, and arrive at the village street.

Leaving the village

I learn about the seriousness, the impact, of this journey. Families are gathered outside their houses to speed the procession on its way. Parents hold up their little ones and children are observing. Grandparents are there. *Doamne ajuta,* they say, as they cross themselves. God help you. All the way through this typically long village people are at their gates. Someone hands them a jar of preserved cherries, another a bottle of brandy. The sheep move forward quickly and eagerly.

The sheep are fresh, and move briskly through the village

At the end of the village, Corina and Nicolae leave us. Stefu and Ioan, with me the foreigner, are on our own with the sheep. Nicolae will join us with the cattle in the morning.

We are moving now between the two villages of Nimaesti and Budureasa. Between them is a huge *pasuna*. These common lands are still a much-used village resource in the outlying parts of Romania which avoided the collectivisation of Communism and the enclosures of England. I love their great wide open grazed expanses.

Nimaesti's herd of cows, each of which belongs to individual families from the village, is approaching as it makes its way home. It is driven as usual by two gypsy children. Stefu and Ioan ensure that the sheep are kept apart from the cattle. They tell me that the cows could injure the sheep with their horns.

Ioan is in front of the long line of sheep, Stefu is behind and I am trying not to do anything wrong or annoying. The flock are moving steadily over the rolling pasture, seeming to know where they are going. Certainly the older sheep have made this journey before.

It has been a hot, clear day. The sunset colours of the clouds are behind us as the sun and the crescent moon set. We are heading broadly east and the way is dark in front. The flock are baaing and maaing as we go, the older ewes and the lambs connecting with each other, and the bells are clanking. Stefu makes a series of different calls as he guides and steers the sheep onwards. He's competent and self-assured, and I much admire his technique as he manages them. In front of us are the steep mountain peaks to which we are heading.

As we pass through the village of Budureasa, I learn how annoying it is when a vehicle approaches. The long line of sheep has to be moved to one side. Some drivers sound the horn irritably and others are patient, giving a short toot as a thank you.

After we leave Budureasa the sheep are given a 15 minute rest in a small field. It is pitch dark now. We are on the asphalt road and have been going for two to three hours. For me, the hardest part lies ahead, the long steep ascent through the forested hills, to Stana de Vale. The word s*tana* means the same as our word *shieling*, a summer settlement for the shepherds. Nowadays, Stana de Vale is a rough and ready ski resort.

Through the forest
Climbing through the forest is like being in a dark dream. We slowly follow the ascending road in total blackness not using the *lanterna,* the torches, so as not to waste the batteries. These are very cost-conscious people. I find my pace, and am at the head of the flock. Luci the mare is there too. It is as though she thinks her job is to lead the flock. I try to find my path in the dense blackness by following her slightly lighter round rear end.

As the hills get steeper, the road begins to make huge loops. The shepherds are not going to follow the winding course if they can take short cuts. At the first serious curve the dogs and Luci seem to know that we will go straight on. Up into the forest we go, where there are terrifying steep drops down to our right. At least they would be terrifying if it were possible to see them but it is totally dark.

Now I decide that saving the light in my lantern is not a priority. Being at the front I shine it so that Stefu, the mare and I can see the path along which we're going. Stefu says *Bun, bun.* He approves.

At the end of each of these short-cuts through the forest there always seems to be a really steep and difficult ascent with loose earth, making it difficult to avoid slipping. Just as I am wondering how much longer this can go on, we reach the asphalt road again.

So the time passes in a sleepy dream. Up, up, up. Sometimes we are on the hard asphalt, sometimes on the short cuts through the forest, hour after hour. There are no rests. An occasional car drives along, but fewer as the night goes on.

At about 2am, Saturday now, it is time for a short rest. There is a small field in an opening in the forest. The men organise the sheep into a group and allow them to graze. I put on all my English woollies and my rainproof gear so that I can rest on the now very damp grass. The men lay out sheets made of strong plastic, which are their much-used and versatile forms of waterproofing, and lie down for an hour.

Plecam, we're leaving again. We make more dream-like ascents until we reach the wooden touristy gateway which announces that we've arrived at the winter sports centre of Stana de Vale. We turn off into what is now coniferous forest and leave the asphalt road permanently for a forest track. Up we go until at about 4.30 am, as the sky is lightening, we arrive at Galbena. Here we are to meet the rest of the family who are arriving by motorised transport.

Next morning, the sheep are moving out of the coniferous forest

The paths across the summer pastures
We're arriving at the area I'd been longing to see, the upland pastures where the shepherds spend the summer. This is the land beyond the forest, *transilvania*, the rolling uplands, nothing between them and the sky; remote, green, lonely, yet connected to the lowlands by the network of people travelling with their animals; who live there in the coolness of the summer, where the grass grows; whereas below in the lowlands the heat dries the grasses and the animals can't thrive.

The lowland pastures are separated from the uplands by the steep forested hillsides which we've climbed through. I am wondering about the time when the Newminster shepherds made their way to the Cheviots; if forests had to be passed through too. Or if by that time most of the trees had been cut down.

The truck with the cattle arrives and they are let out. Nicolae and the cattle will walk from now on as the truck can't manage the path. Lie arrives driving the tractor which is pulling the loaded *caruta* on which Florica is balancing. They had left home early in the morning while we were walking with the sheep.

Off we go. Lie and Florica go on ahead on the tractor. Stefu and I lead the sheep now with Ioan behind. Nicolae follows with his seven cattle. There is a cow with her three-week old calf, a tiny adorable creature, and five young heifers of varying sizes. As the calf is so young they travel slowly and generally are behind the sheep by some distance.

I have a map which doesn't much impress these people who know the way so well. It shows the route from Galbena heading south east and then north east, crossing many rounded peaks. Virful Bodohie is 1654 metres high, Carligatele 1694 metres, Virful Britei 1759 metres and finally our destination Virful Micau at 1640 metres. Our starting point was at about 500 metres. There is a modern marked tourist trail here, a blue streak painted on rocks, which follows this ancient route.

At 10 am we all meet up at *Fontana Rece*, Cold Fountain, which bubbles out of the ground, and have a good breakfast. I am told it is another six hours walking. We've been on the go for fifteen hours and the family suggest I ride on the *caruta*. Certainly not, I say, refusing to admit I might be tired. The best bit lies ahead. They shake their heads. *Ai ai ai. Saizeci si sapte!* Sixty-seven years old!

They are very accepting people. The tractor goes on ahead, taking Ioan, and leaving just me in front and Stefu at the rear of the flock. Nicolae is always some distance in the rear, at the pace of the calf. It is hard. It is heavenly. There seems to be an endless series of green hills, steep and upward, steeply down again, rolling, one after the other.

I am gradually learning what the lead shepherd needs to do. Luci the mare and I go in front. She is quite free to go where she wants and diverts whenever she finds some tasty grasses. But usually she likes to be with me. She'll catch me up and nudge my back. We become very friendly. So I call the sheep as I've observed the shepherds do: *Hoi hoi hoi*, and they seem to respond and know what is expected. We are all mammals after all and have some similar body language. Their ears prick forward, we have eye contact, and I am encouraging them onwards.

Luci leads the way. She and the sheep snatch a mouthful of grass as they go. They have left the forest and are on the mountain pastures

I plod along fairly slowly. Sheep and people are getting tired. The pace is probably about two miles per hour and manageable. The thing is to put one foot in front of another and not to think about how much further it is.

Thus I am learning how the shepherds and the sheep work together in Romania, as it seems to me quite different from in the UK. Do these shepherds really lead their sheep, as in the biblical sense? I think yes, more or less, they do.

63

The shepherds have dogs but they are not working collies like ours. The big woolly dogs are to guard the sheep from wolves and thieves. They act independently, travelling alongside. They don't let you touch them. They are not pets but more like co-travellers. There are six dogs accompanying this *traseu*. Vultur, Codru, Dorina and Urs are the guard dogs. They look rather like a mixture between Old English sheepdogs and Alsatians. Lena is a pup and she is travelling on the *caruta*. There is also Boga, a terrier-like dog, who is a pet. He insists on walking with Nicolae though his little legs must be tiring. He doesn't help at all with the sheep.

Thus the shepherds handle the sheep without the help of dogs, keeping the sheep in their group. Stragglers are rounded up or sometimes they just catch up by themselves. No real straying is tolerated and the sheep are well enough used to the routine to know they have to rejoin the flock when the shepherds threaten them with the sticks.

Stefu calls to them constantly, communicating with them as we progress.

My *Hoi hoi hoi* is becoming more fluent and Stefu seems to appreciate my help. I'm a little stiff and very glad to have my stick. At the front, if I'm not sure which way to go at any point, I look back and Stefu raises his stick, pointing out if I should turn left or right or go straight on. The line of sheep is too long for shouting. This silent stick signalling is very satisfying.

At a crossroads in the mountain paths we rest for a while, and Nicolae catches up with his cattle. Suddenly a mountain biker appears in colourful regalia and has long conversations with Nicolae. He is a modern young man from the city. He is amazed at Nicolae's story about spending three months in the mountains. Nicolae encourages him to come to his cabin at Micau later. He knows that tourists pay extra good prices for his freshly-made cheese.

The last kilometre or two are stretching ahead. There is a big wooden cross on the top of the next hill. It is not far to Micau now. At last, we look down on the *cabana*, the cabin, with some other wooden buildings and some fenced sheepfolds. Florica is waiting for us, smiling and happy. It is about 6 pm. The *traseu* has taken about 23 hours.

Stefu and the sheep arrive at the mountain hut after at the end of the 23 hour, 59 kilometre uphill walk

The cabin is beside a spring from which a little stream trickles away between blue forget-me-nots and golden buttercups. We are on the grassy uplands with views down over blue mountains and dark coniferous forests. The sheep are tired and hungry, grazing ravenously. They are moved into the sheepfold to be milked. They had missed the morning milking so this is a priority.

When it is done the men have to re-roof the cabin with plastic as it has been damaged over the winter. This involves clambering up onto the roof, and much hammering.

Making the cheese

Florica has to get the cheese-making process started. Not a drop of this precious milk will be wasted. The milk is strained through cloths, poured into huge plastic bowls, and the chemical rennet is added. Soon it begins to coagulate and then it is hung up in bags from the roof. The whey drips into buckets below.

Next morning, the first batch of cheese is hanging up and the next batch will soon be ready.

Even though everyone is tired no-one stops for a moment. Except for me. I just collapse on the one shared bed in the cabin among the thousands of mosquitoes.

The family don't sleep in the hut. The bed is for visitors. They have to watch the valuable sheep at night. On three sides of the square wooden fold are rectangular pods, sleeping shelters, full of blankets and covered with plastic sheets. They face in to the sheep. The dogs too are ever vigilant. There are always tales of wolves trying to take a sheep. This would have been the same with the Newminster shepherds in Northumberland.

In the morning I wake to the clank of metal containers and the plip plop of the dripping milk into the buckets. The round cheeses are hanging from the roof. Lie will take those home and come back a week later for more.

The Candea family Stefu, Nicolae, Florica, Lie and Ioan, with Lena the guard dog puppy

Florica and the author each wearing a bitusha, *the enveloping sheepskin coats important for coping with cold and windy weather in the mountains*

....

Later, as I make my way back down to the lowlands, I wonder how much longer this tradition will survive. There are flocks from other villages on their own upland pastures. I see two men in traditional shepherds' dress, with plaid shawls folded over their shoulders, and wearing pointed hats. A horse-drawn *caruta* is following another path upward, too far away for me to make contact.

There are also abandoned huts and sheepfolds where intrusive giant sorrel plants can be found. Juniper is taking over where the grass is no longer being grazed. One problem is that the now-regular tractor journeys are damaging the track. At a particularly tricky steep place, there is so much erosion that Lie's driving has to be death-defying. On the way up I'd observed Florica holding on for dear life as she was thrown to and fro. If this damage continues, it may make the upland pastures inaccessible.

European regulations too must eventually have an impact. Hygiene standards of cheese-making in the hills wouldn't pass any EU inspections. But for now, Florica and her young sons are doing well enough. The family has chosen to continue the way of life they have inherited, using the seasons and the village's uplands to maximise production from their flock; just as the monks did, long long ago in Northumberland, when they moved the flocks to the hills. This is the next adventure.

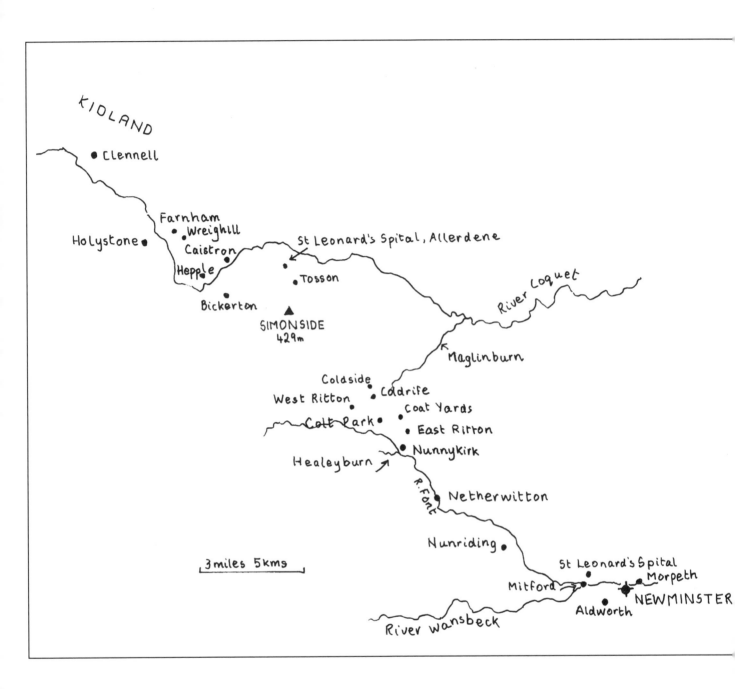

Following the flocks and herds from Newminster to Kidland, according to the charters. Upstream along the Font valley, over the watershed into the Coquet valley and upstream to Clennell

5 The road to Kidland

Gathering the flocks

If you had been driving into Morpeth from the Mitford direction on a June morning in 2012, you might have seen three monk-like figures pushing their loaded bicycles away from the green mounds of the buried Newminster.

Mary, Rosie and I are following in the footsteps of the flocks of sheep, making their way towards the grassy ranges of the Cheviot hills. We are wearing our white wool monks' habits, pulling the hoods over our faces to keep out the cool morning wind and rolling the skirts up into the girdles around our waists to keep them out of the way when we pedal. We are planning to take about a week on this trek, two or three days getting there and three or four in the hills.

The Wansbeck river is flowing on our right along its woodland course, and to our left is the abandoned channel which took the gurgling water to the abbey. This is where the monks had their sheepfold, their *bercaria*, in the flat riverside haughs between the lands of the de Merlays of Morpeth and the Bertrams of Mitford. This is where the sheep would have been gathered for the great summer trek to the hills and the excitement that went with it.

There would have been children, boys and women, the shepherds with their sticks and the semi-feral dogs lurching around. Noise, excitement and yet control. The brown-clothed lay brothers would be very much in charge, calling, organising. There would be associated carts and pack-ponies carrying the goods needed for the summer in the hills. The sheep would be restless; the older ewes hungry for the juicy grasses that they knew awaited them. And once the sheep were assembled and blessed, off they would go with urgency and energy.

As long ago as the 1180s, the Umfravill lords of Redesdale had granted land on their Cheviot moors to the monks of Newminster. This land was used for summer grazing grounds and flocks and herds from the lowland granges would be driven up to the hills, along routes where all the rights of way were established. This seasonal movement of people with their animals is called *transhumance*. Once in the hills, the herders would settle in for a couple of months in their shelters which in Northumberland are called *shielings*. This has all long disappeared in England but lingering later in parts of Scotland. It still takes place in some European countries although the animals may be moved by motor transport. Tracking the transhumance route from Newminster to the Kidland area of the Cheviots was what Rosie, Mary and I were going to do. We would be thinking ourselves into the role of the people who went with the flocks, the monks perhaps, but certainly the lay brothers and their servants.

We know well that there will not be many monuments remaining to be seen from the time the flocks passed by in the twelfth and thirteenth centuries and the landscape will be different in many ways. But in this area of rural Northumberland, remote from the well-visited tourist areas, we will follow the ancient ways where we can. The rivers and streams are still flowing in the valleys that the monks and shepherds knew. The rise and fall of the landscape, with steep slopes to push up and sail down on our bicycles, is the same. So is the unpredictable weather.

The period with which we are principally concerned on this trek is from the foundation of the monastery until the invasion of Scotland by Edward I in 1296. I have a folder full of information to enlighten our journey, much from the cartulary. The other two sources are Hodgson's histories from the 1820s and 1830s for the first part of the trek and Madeleine Hope Dodds' Volume 15 of *A History of Northumberland* from 1940 for the second.

Our chosen course is to head north westerly following the course of the Font river, then up and over the watershed between it and the Coquet river. Starting at Newminster, we will be in the footsteps of the flocks from the abbey's home farm. Any that came from the other granges of Ulgham or Horton or Sharplaw would join the route at suitable places. The herders would all know how far they could travel in a day and the places where they would rest for the night. The journey to the hills was about 30 miles from Newminster. They could do it in two days or three perhaps.

....

Shortly after leaving the abbey, we know that there was once a little settlement called Aldworth lying on the land beyond the southern wooded horizon. This is the mysterious place which appears in the cartulary in Gradus III, just after Morpeth, among a few very old and unusual charters from the Bertrams. The only clue about Aldworth's location comes from the mention of the boundaries between Aldworth and Edington, a farm which still exists to the south of Mitford.

These charters concern the chaplains of Mitford and show us that in those early days the clergy were not celibate. The chaplains had sons. Fowler in his introduction to the cartulary tells us this:

> Under the head of Aldworth, p 107, we find some indications that there were married clergy in the north of England in the twelfth century. It is sometimes stated that priests who were fathers of sons must have become so previous to ordination, but there is abundance of evidence that marriage of the clergy was quite usual in the eleventh century.[70]

In the first charter in this section, Roger Bertram I presented land to his chaplain Richard son of Baldwin:

> … terram de Aldeworth del west del chymyn quod vadit per mediam villam de Aldworthe, per rectas divisas quae sunt inter Aldworth et Ydyngton …

> … land of Aldworth to the west of the lane that goes through half the vill of Aldworth, along the straight boundaries that are between Aldworth and Edington … (p107)

There is a charitable request by Roger Bertram I some time around 1170 to his chaplain, and a statement about the rent:

> … pascendo semel in anno centum pauperes pro animabus patrum meorum et omnium antecessorum meorum, et reddendo mihi et heredibus meis xiij d. ad oblacionem ad festum Sancti Thomae apostoli.

> … feeding annually one hundred poor people for the soul of my father and all my ancestors, and rendering to me and my heirs an offering of thirteen pence at the feast of Saint Thomas the apostle. (p107)

In the next charter, Roger Bertram II grants to Newminster the land that his grandfather gave to Richard son of Baldwin. He relinquishes payment to him of the thirteen pence annually and gives precise details of what the abbey is to give to the hundred poor people:

> Et sciendum quod ego Rogerus, caritatis intuitu remisi et relaxavi et quietam clamavi … xiij d … in pascend. centum pauperibus in die Santae Katerinae … duas cacas avenae et duo allecia ad portam Novi Mon. …

> And thus I Roger charitably remit and quitclaim … thirteen pence … for the feasting of a hundred Paupers on St Katherine's day … two oatcakes and two herrings at the gate of New Minster … (pp107-108)

We're travelling towards Mitford where the Bertrams had their hill-top castle next to the Wansbeck river, probably built of wood like that of the de Merlays in the earliest days. The route to the Cheviots follows the Font rather than the Wansbeck, so we won't pass it by.

---

[70] Fowler, p xvii

As we approach Mitford, there is a steep hill on our right with a signpost to St Leonard's. There was once a chapel and a spital here. Its history is a little vague. What is a *spital*? Not a hospital as we know it, perhaps, but more of a resting place for pilgrims which could be useful for those visiting the tomb of St Robert at Newminster, of which we'll learn more in a later chapter.

Hodgson tells us that it was founded by William Bertram in the time of Henry I (1100-1135). By 1324, he writes, it was wasted. At some point, the abbot of Newminster obtained it. In an inquest in 1377, St Leonard's Hospital held 40 acres from the manor of Mitford including the "Fouse Bridge". "But the abbot of Newminster, long before that time, had converted them to his purposes and then still occupied them".[71]

Newminster's cartulary contains several charters from between 1491 and 1493 concerning St Leonard's hospital and the chapel. In 1489 the abbot of Newminster and the prior of Brinkburn were agreeing boundaries there with the master of the hospital. One of the arbitrators was Lord Henry Percy of Northumberland, the guardian of the east and middle marches along the border between England and Scotland. It was decided that Newminster would pay four shillings a year to Brinkburn (p249).

In 1491, Henry Gray granted two waste chapels to abbot Robert of Newminster, one being St Cuthbert's at Bockenfield, a few miles north of Newminster, and the other St Leonard's near Mitford (p249).

There were several disputes and at one stage St Cuthbert's was apportioned to Brinkburn and St Leonard's to Newminster. This charter is one of the very few in English:

> … the said Abbott and Couent shall haue and enioy to thame and ther successours for eu' the said waste chapell called saynt leonardes bysyde Myttfurth wt oon cotage in Benrige … (p251)

All these dealings were at a later period than the early centuries of the abbey which we are mainly considering now.

The shepherds and the flocks would need to cross the Font river here at Mitford. Possibly the "Fouse Bridge" mentioned by Hodgson was there in the later centuries. Previous to that this had always been a place where the rivers had to be forded. So splashing through the water the sheep and shepherds would go.

---

[71] Hodgson, Part II/ii, p 74

We follow old minor roads and footpaths towards Nunriding. This is the land controlled by the sisters of Holystone priory further along our way. We are imagining the nuns checking their boundaries and supervising their shepherds; and the peasant women working for them as they milked and cared for their sheep.

Nunriding: the place where the nuns cleared the woodlands. Here is Hodgson again:

> Nunriding has its name from having been *assarted* or *ridded* of wood by the nuns of Holystone, to whom it had been given by Roger Bertram the first, under the name of Baldwineswood ... Roger Bertram had granted common of pasture to the nuns of Holystone on the common of Newton and Throphill, which grant Henry the Third confirmed at Newcastle in 1225.[72]

It seems unlikely that the nuns themselves would have cut down trees and cleared the woodlands but rather they, like the monks, would have engaged the local people. Once *ridded* of trees the land could be used for growing crops, and sheep and cattle would be able to graze on the nearby commons. The Newminster shepherds and lay brothers would have known that they were passing through the lands belonging to the nuns, just as we do.

An *assarted* field, with its curved boundary implying medieval ploughing patterns, is on our right. The woodland beside it, flecked with light under the bright green oak leaves of early summer, fills us with a sense of time gone by. This is a remnant of ancient landscape. The oaks are huge, the silver birch vast and rugged on the fringes. There are gigantic many-stemmed hollies. We make a list of the woodland flora:

> herb robert, wood sorrel, violet, wood aven, bluebell, sanicle, hedge woundwort

We pass by Longshaws farm, the name itself having captured a glimpse of the older landscape, the element *shaw* meaning *wood* or *copse,* from old English *sceaga*[73]. The route goes downhill to Netherwitton. Near here there is a hamlet called Longwitton. Hodgson suggests that the name of Witton, which appears from the time of the foundation charter, could come from *wood town*; and this is indeed an area of woodland along the winding valley sides. He comments:

> Ranulph de Merlay, when he founded the abbey of Newminster, was careful that it should not in future times be destitute of a spot well adapted to the growth of timber.[74]

Soon, we are sitting on the bench on Netherwitton village green encircled by purple columbine and golden buttercups. Attracted by our woolly monks' outfits, Pamellia who lives just there brings us lovely hot cups of tea. She's interested in our transhumance trek. She did just as exciting things at our age and now she is in her 80s. We roll back our wool habits as the sun shines on us and then pull them back around us as it goes behind the clouds. The breeze is strong and cold. We wonder what the weather will do to us later.

Next we cycle along the narrow road to Nunnykirk, just beyond Netherwitton. What does this word mean? The church of the nuns? Which nuns if so?

Northumberland County Council's Heritage Environment Record ID 10821 gives various sources of information, from which I've taken the following:

Hodgson wrote in 1827:

> This place was comprised in Ranulph de Merlay's grant of Ritton to Newminster, the abbot of which house built a chapel, tower and other edifices here, all traces of which are now gone.[75]

---

[72] Hodgson, Part II/ii, p 74
[73] Allen Mawer, *The Place Names of Northumberland and Durham,* CUP, 1920, pp 136 and 238
[74] Hodgson, part 2, vol I, p312
[75] Hodgson, part 2, vol I, pp329 – 330

C J Bates suggests that Nunnykirk might have been the site of the nunnery *Vetadun*, mentioned in Bede's *Ecclesiastical History* which he wrote in 731 AD.[76] But after extensive discussions with place name experts and historians, I have learned that this is not correct, and that *Vetadun* is Watton, seven miles north of Beverley in North Yorkshire.

Returning to the Heritage Evironment Record, C W Orde, the owner of the site reported in 1957:

> Nunnykirk was completely rebuilt by my grandfather in 1810. I have never heard of the remains of underground foundations and human bones supposed to have been found on the site. There are no traces of chapel, grange and tower to be seen anywhere.[77]

Nunnykirk does appear in Newminster's dissolution documents where it is described as a grange, although it was obviously poor with a very small income. In a document of 1547, there is a mention of a tower.[78] In the period up to 1296, there is no evidence to suggest a tower. that I have seen. It would probably have been built in the later period of English and Scottish conflicts.

The Heritage Environment Record also mentions the Abbess's Well or Monks' Well but it was found to be a small stone-lined cist set into the Font river, recorded in 1957. The name could be a later invention and does not add anything useful to our knowledge.

All this does not rule out that there was an Anglo-Saxon nunnery there; it is just that so far no evidence seems to have been found. Thus, reluctantly, I am unable to suggest that there were any certain monuments such as a chapel or a tower in our period which the shepherds and the lay brothers would have seen as they passed by with the flocks and herds.

There is slim possibility, though, that a most outstanding historic cross could have been.

We know from the charters that boundary descriptions often include stone crosses. On the modern OS maps a *cross* is marked, apparently on the opposite side of the Font river from the present-day Nunnykirk school at approximately NZ 080 926. When I was planning this trek, I had been pleased to think that we might pass it. But on enquiring I learned that the cross is at the Great North Museum in Newcastle. At some time in the past it had been built into a cottage wall, probably as just a useful piece of stonework. When the cottage was being demolished in the 1850s, it was placed in a corner of the stackyard. It was acquired by the Newcastle Society of Antiquaries in 1976. It is now on prominent display at the museum where I went to draw it.

This beautiful cross is known to date from the early 9th century. On the front side is a design of winding vines combined with a pair of birds and what looks like a pair of horses. The sides and rear are decorated with interlocking vines. It stands to a height of 4 feet 6 inches and comprises the shaft only.[79] It would have had a stone cross on its head and how wonderful it would have been to see it.

No-one seems to know exactly where it had been standing originally. And yet, there is a tantalising clue. In one of Roger de Merlay's charters confirming all the boundaries around Ritton we find this:

> … concedo, et confimo, scilicet, apud Ritton ab eo loco ubi Fauleyburn cadit in Funt versus north usque ad moram, et inde in transversum usque ad Standenstane, et inde versus northwest usque ad Harrecars …

---

[76] C J Bates, Heritage Environment Record Northumberland County Council, ID 10821
[77] Oral, C W Orde (owner) Nunnykirk, 10.1.57
[78] Assignment by Richard Tyrrell to Thomas Grey, Surtees Society Vol 66, 1876, Newminster cartulary appendix IV, pp 309 - 316
[79] Heritage Environment Record, Northumberland County Council, ID 10822,

… I concede, and confirm, namely, at Ritton from the place where Healeyburn comes into the Font towards the north as far as the moor, and from there crossing as far as the Standingstone, and from there towards the northwest as far as Harrecars … (p8)

So there was a standing stone here, near where the Healeyburn joins the Font river, which is just a little to the south of Nunnykirk school. Could this cross have been the standing stone? The shepherds and the lay brothers might have passed it by, using it as a waymarker. I like to think they did.

Rosie, Mary and I arrive at the turnoff to Nunnykirk School for Dyslexia. Everything is quiet. Where were all the children, we wonder. We come to the classical building with its stone columns and pull the bell.

Out comes a friendly woman who tells us that her name is Carole Hodgson, and that she is the headmistress. She shows no surprise at seeing three monk-like figures with bicycles at her door. It is Friday and all the children have gone home for the weekend. She tells us about their special work for seriously dyslexic children and says that she has taken them to see the Nunnykirk Cross in Newcastle. She later photocopied and posted to me two archaeological reports which had been made when they were planning to build additions to the school. The reports did not add any hard information to what I had already been able to find out, unfortunately.

....

The large beasts of Coltpark

"An ice cream would come in very handy", says my sister-monk Rosie. Mary agrees. I was forever getting out my files of information as we ambled along and they patiently absorbed what they wanted to. But the needs of the body as well as the mind must be attended to and we have found a little shop at a caravan site beside the Font river. She and Mary lick their purchases happily and it is a good thing they have this energy boost. The next part of our day's journey is up a very steep hill to Coltpark farm where we plan to camp for the night.

Rising up the hills from the caravan park we find ourselves amid the long wide views, with the smell of the moorland and the sheep grazing on the old pastures. The new wind turbines do not disconcert me at all. We can see westward towards the headlands of the Font, east to the sea, and south over the up-and-down land of marginal hill farms and tree-lined back roads.

The place names here have echoes of our medieval ancestors, lost words, old days and ways; Hesleyhurst, Maglin Burn, Morrellhirst, Healeyburn.

Between West Ritton and East Ritton, this open landscape was of great economic importance to the monks. There are a few surviving records of what seems to be the grasping of land rights by the abbot of Newminster from local people.

The cartulary records a case where John, son of Robert, from Rothbury was obliged to make concessions to the abbot (p 10). This is an agreement "before the King's justiciaries at Newcastle about pasture at West Ritton", according to Fowler's marginal notes. Madeleine Hope Dodds made this interpretation:

> In 1225, John son of Robert agreed that the abbot of Newminster should have pasture appertaining to his manor of West Ritton, from the place where Wyteden joined the Font, up the Font to the highway leading to Heselden, and running north and by the same highway to Heltantre, going down to Healeyburn and from Healeyburn to the road that runs south to Crokestanes by the old road to Maghild and by Maghild to Maghilead; this pasture should be for all the abbot's cattle and plough horses, and the abbot should also estover (have the right to gather wood) in the same area by view of the forester for firewood, fencing and building, and the way to his quarry at Aldrecheastell.[80]

She points out that John was able to reserve the right of pasture for his own cattle within these boundaries but not for the cattle of the men of Rothbury. So he got something out of it.

The story continues. In 1263 the abbot complained about the servants of Roger son of Roger of Rothbury who were depriving him of 1000 acres of his right of pasture in Hesleyhurst. He won his case. The defendants appealed in 1266 but again the verdict was in the abbot's favour.[81] It was not until the time of Robert son of Roger that the issue was settled, probably in the 1270s, when he was obliged to grant the disputed rights to the abbot.[82]

Hodgson reports a later case where the abbot didn't get away with it:

> … the abbot claimed free warren, at the assizes, in Newcastle, in 1294, by grant of Edw. the First, in 1290; but Greystock and Somerville, who married the heiresses of the baron of Morpeth, proving that their ancestor had granted him no such privilege, the jury gave their verdict against his claim, and also ordered him to pull down the fences of a very large wood, which he had inclosed at East Ritton; and also of a great park which he had made there to keep large beasts in, and which, probably from the use it was first put to, obtained its present name of Ritton *Colt-park*.[83]

Free warren means the right to hunt small game; but in this case it has connotations of enclosure of land.[84]

Hodgson's notion that the name of Colt-park is related to the *large beasts* which were enclosed there is intriguing. Coltpark, Coldrife, Coat Yards, Coldside; all four farm names still survive here.

We are nearly there. Rosie, Mary and I push up the hill, twenty steps at a go, a stop to admire the view and another twenty steps. The monks are tiring.

"Hallo there. Are you lost?" calls out the farmer at Coltpark.

---

[80] Madeleine Hope Dodds, A History of Northumberland, Vol 15, p 353 and Newminster Cartulary p 10 – 11
[81] Dodds, pp 353 - 354
[82] Dodds, p 354
[83] Hodgson, Vol II ii, p 322 (cd this be part III?)
[84] wikipedia.org/wiki/Free_warren

He's joking. He'd already heard on the countryside bush telegraph that we were heading this way. Someone who'd chatted with us at Netherwitton had been shopping in Rothbury, and met him and told him that the monks were coming.

My vague tales about the monks of Newminster in the 1200s are usually too remote in time to trigger anything other than raised eyebrows to those who kindly listen to me. If it wasn't for the Newminster cartulary, and my focussed researches in Hodgson and elsewhere, I wouldn't have had any idea either about the significance of the name Coltpark. Serving us tea and cakes, Neil and Leigh Purvis, the managers of Coltpark farm, patiently listen to our stories. And then Neil takes us down to a field where we had pre-arranged with them to camp. We pass the fields with rolling ridge and furrow next to their farm and then push the bikes down to a sheltered spot under some ancient oak trees, next to a tiny burn.

"Oh dear me!" says Rosie. "The tent pegs aren't in the bag!" Black clouds are alternating with glorious sunshine to the west. As she can't put the tent up, Rosie organises an improvised sleeping arrangement using the tent's fabric as waterproof outer covers. Mary has a tent, I have brought a plastic survival bag rather than a tent; and thus we prepare our beds for the night. We are planning to camp for the first two nights and to stay in Clennell Hall later. Rosie and Mary cook the lentil stew while I go off again to look at the landscape. The full moon is rising behind the oak trees as I return and the sun lowering in the west. We settle down to sleep with our midgy hats over our faces. Yes, there are midges. But still, we feel, this is indeed a lovely place.

....

Until, in the night, plop plop plop from the oak leaves above us. It is starting. Gentle sweet smelling raindrops at first. Gradually the rivulets accumulate into streams, passing under my arrangement but directly into Rosie's.

"Clennell Hall, where are you?" she shouts. "Mary, I'm coming in!"

And she dives head first into Mary's tent while I giggle under the shelter of my bivvy-bag.

In the morning we pack up our soaking gear in a rough and ready fashion, and struggle up the field through the deep soggy grass to the road to find Mary's bike has a puncture. The back wheel of course. Off comes all the baggage. All to be done before any warm drinks can be thought of; and with more rain threatening.

On the way up to the brow of the hill beyond Coltpark is the place I call Juliana's View. It is pouring with rain now, with a driving wind, so we don't stop.

But in decent weather, from here, looking back south and east, we can see the lands of her dowry; Ritton and Witton to the boundary with Wingates, the land gradually lowering towards Morpeth where she lived after her marriage, and Newminster Abbey. This is gentle fertile woodland and farms, the winding valley of the Font river as it flows past the Rittons and Nunnykirk. Had she ever travelled this way to see the land that was her own? Had she accompanied the men on horseback who perambulated her land, which she was signing away? If she was like Rosie, Mary and me, she would have wanted to. Perhaps she put up an argument with her father and her brother. All we can do is ponder.

....

In the Coquet valley

We're moving into a new world. The rain has stopped, miraculously. We pause on the brow of the hill just beyond Lordenshaws hillfort. We've left the Font behind us and are looking ahead to the hills where the sheep and cattle spent the summer. The shepherds and monks who've done this route before would be able to point out the hill of Kidland which the great de Umfravill lords made available for Newminster. It is just a little to the west of the great flat hill of Cheviot on the skyline. The heather-clad Simonside range is on our left. We will now follow the course of the Coquet river upstream all the way to the hills.

It's a wonderful free-wheel down the steep escarpment. How we long for a morning cup of coffee after the wet night, the puncture and the pouring rain. We are so damp. The kind bed and breakfast lady at Tosson Farm agrees to brew us some coffee. She lets us sit amid her scarlet geraniums.

This seems to be just the right place for a centre of hospitality after tackling the watershed hills between the Coquet and the Font. In fact there was just such a place, near here, at Allerdene.

Once again it is a hospital of St Leonard but there are no material remains. All we know about it is from documentary sources and that is little. As long ago as 1939, the writer R N Hadcock felt able to write:

> Apparently it came into the possession of Newminster, in which case it was probably used as a hospice, being on the road between Newminster and the monks' estates in Kidland.[85]

Further evidence is from Dodds:

> It appears probable that the hospital was founded by the family of Richard Chartenay and Maud his wife who were married between 1212 and 1229 ... The whole manor of Hepple was eventually united in the possession of the Ogles, and the hospital must have been given by some member of the family to Newminster.[86]

Dodds also records that the hospital appears in 1553 in the former possessions of the monastery after the dissolution, under the tenure of the widow Swandon, with associated land. Thus in some form or other it survived for a few centuries.

---

[85] R N Hadcock, Archaeologia Aeliana, 4 series, no 16, 1939, p 181, cited in Heritage Environment Record 2843
[86] Madeleine Hope Dodds, Northumberland County History, Vol 15, p 337

The hermits of Caistron

In the early 1200s there were some hermits in Coquetdale. On 27 January 1247, the cartulary records that John son of John of Caistron, for the health of the souls of his wife Katherine, their sons and all their successors, granted land to two brothers:

> ... Beato Johanni de Maydeneley et fratri Hugoni de Hepes et suis successoribus vij acras terrae circa Maydeneleyam, quarum duae acrea seminabuntur multociens per dictum fratrem Hugonem ante hanc cartae meae confimacionem, et v acras residuae de novo seminabuntur juxta dictas ij acras ...

> ... Blessed John of Maidenley and his brother Hugo of Hepes and their successors seven acres of land around Maidenley, which two acres of arable land the brother Hugo confirmed many times, and five acres of new arable land next to the said two acres ... (p138)

In the next charter we have verification that Hugh was a hermit and that he later granted his land to the abbey of Newminster:

> Omnibus, etc. Frater Hugo heremita de Meyndenley, sal. Noveritis me ded. conc. et. p. c. m. conf. Deo et B. M. Abb. et mon. Novi Mon. et eorum successoribus locum de Meydenley et totam terram quam habui in territorio de Kestern ...

> To all, etc. Brother Hugo the hermit of Maidenley, greetings. Notice that I give, concede and through this my charter confirm to God and the Blessed Mary the abbot and monastery of Newminster and their successors the place of Maidenley and all the land that I have in Caistron ... (p139)

Nowadays, Caistron is known for its great gravel extractions in the bed of the Coquet river. This has resulted in huge ponds. Only a few bird watchers and fishermen now come to these secluded wetlands. As we push our bikes along the off-road tracks where the channels meander back into the Coquet we see what looks like a little hermit's shelter.

Beside the flood-strewn roots of a willow tree is evidence of human activity. Someone has brought an old carpet and there is a wooden box which has been made into a kind of table and cupboard. As we are thinking about Blessed John and Brother Hugo, we romantically imagine that this is a hideaway for a modern hermit, meditating perhaps in the silence of the secluded land. But no. We find the pieces of a cardboard jigsaw puzzle and then a store of empty gun cartridges. We decide it is probably a hunters' lair.

Thomas of Bickerton

Beyond the ponds is Bickerton, which has its own section in the cartulary in Gradus III, and it is there that we settle in a golden field of buttercups for a rest. The west wind is now battering us remorselessly. Bright white clouds are rushing furiously across the sky. We know that we must dry our damp tents and sleeping bags, so we tie them to the metal bars of a gate and the fence posts where they fly like flags in the wind. We sprawl at eye-level with the buttercups to make hot drinks, trying to protect our little stove from the wind, and I read a story about Thomas of Bickerton to Rosie and Mary which I've extracted from Dodds' history. He was living here at around the same time as the hermits:

> Thomas, son of Hugh Bickerton, was living in 1246 -56. He was a man of overbearing behaviour who in 1255 imprisoned three women of Bickerton, Emma who had an infant son Cecil, Edith and Christiana, in a cell from Sunday to Wednesday without food or drink and then sent them to Newcastle gaol for stealing from him a bushel of malt; in consequence Christiana and the baby died. Emma and Edith were tried at the assize of 1256 and brought a counteraction against Thomas. They were acquitted, the jury putting the responsibility for the theft conveniently on the dead Christiana, and Thomas was fined 60 shillings.[87]

---

[87] Dodds, p 387

The unsavoury-sounding Thomas granted rights of way through his land to the monks of Newminster:

> Thomas de Bikerton, salutem. … conc. et p. c. m. conf. mon. et fratibus No. Mon. et eor. hom. sufficientem viam et liberam summagiis, cariagiis, bigis, carectis, averiis, et ovibus eorum per terram meam, … ex australi parte de Coket usque ad Hespricheford, et sic usque ad crucem lapideam …

> Thomas of Bickerton, greetings. … I concede and by this my charter confirm to the monks and brothers of Newminster and their men adequate roadway and free passage for carriages, two-horsed chariots, carts, cattle and sheep through my land … from the south side of the Coquet as far as Hespricheford, and from there to the stone cross … (p160)

What a noisy, busy procession it must have been, clittering and clattering, baaing and bellowing and barking.

Rights of way

The Bickerton section of the cartulary is five pages long and all the charters refer to right of passage through the land. This is clear evidence that we are on the right route between Newminster and Kidland. Following the two from Thomas are grants by other donors. Although these landowners obviously have some influence and control, they are not from the lordly baronial families. This one actually uses the word *transeuncia* which is the closest word I've found in the charters to *transhumance*. Here are the relevant selections:

> Petrus dictus le Gras de Thirnum et Johanna uxor ejus, Will. de Everingham manens in eadam villa et Mariota uxor ejus, salutem in Domino. … Concedimus eciam pro nobis et her. n. dictis abb. et conv. ut omnia animalia sua … transeauncia in praed. terris nostris …

> Peter called the Gras of Thirnum and Johanna his wife, William of Everingham living in that village and Mariota his wife, greetings in the Lord … We grant also for us and our heirs to the said abbey and convent all their animals … transhumance through our aforementioned lands … (p160)

The next charters from John son of Stephen of Thirnum and Richard son of Roger of Horsley both specifically point out that the route is to the *mora de Chiuiot,* the moor of Cheviot.

Then come two granting free passage from John of Sharperton and Robert of Hepple which include the phrase *extra bladum et partum.* This means *outside wheatfield and meadow,* and frequently appears in charters which allow passage through land. It is to ensure that the flocks and herds are kept under control so that they don't damage crops. Another follows from Luke Taileboys who gives free right of way through all his barony of Hepple.

The last charter in this section is an agreement between the abbot and Thomas of Clennell in 1228. In this one, the abbot takes the initiative. He seems to be making peace after some difficulties.

> Anno Domini millesimo cc° xx° viii° ad Assumpcionem B. M. in hunc modum reformata est pax inter Abb. et Conv. No. Mo. ex una parte, et Thomam de Clenill ex altera de omnibus controversiis et querelis inter eos motis, scilicet, quod dicti abb. et conv. concesserunt eidem Thomae caritative participacionem oracionum et omn. bonorum spiritualium quae fient in domo No. Mo. in perpetuum, et cum in fata decesserit, sepulturam cum monachis si voluerit et plenarium servicium sicud monacho.

> In the year 1228 at the Assumption of the Blessed Mary in this way peace was restored concerning all quarrels between the Abbot and Convent of Newminster on the one side, and Thomas of Clennell on the other of all quarrels between them, namely, that the said abbot and convent conceded kindly to the same Thomas inclusion in the prayers and all good spiritual benefits that will be done by the house of Newminster in perpetuity, and when he has gone to his death, burial with the monks if he wishes, and the full service just as for a monk. (p163)

In return, the abbey gets from Thomas the right of free way for his men and carriages:

> … in eundo versus abbathiam et inde redeundo a villa de Clenill ascendendo per vallem et aquam de Alewent versus Kidland …

> … in going towards the abbey and returning from the village of Clennell going up through the valley and water of the Alwent towards Kidland … (p163)

A set of fines is then laid out for incursions into cornfields and meadows:

> … detur ad parchagium pro xx averiis unus denarius, et pro xl ovibus j denarius, et pro v porcis j denarius, et pro x equabus cum uno stalione iiij denarius, et pro x equabus sine stalione j denarius …

> … let there be given a fine for straying by twenty cattle one penny, and for forty sheep one penny, and for five pigs one penny, and for ten horses with one stallion four pence, and for ten horses without a stallion one penny … (p164)

There are not many mentions of pigs in the charters. So here we learn that they too were herded through the countryside.

As the monks have some land in nearby Kidland, this agreement also applies to Thomas's animals encroaching on the abbey's land:

> Similater si averia praedicti T. vel heredum suorum inparchata fuerint in pastura monachorum vel inventa in prato vel blado eorum simili taxacione excessus corrigatur.

> In the same way if Thomas's animals or those of his heirs encroach on the pasture of the monks or are found in their pastures or cornfields the same fines will be paid. (p164)

With all these wayleave agreements, the monks had guaranteed access through this crucial length of the Coquet valley between the Simonside hills and the Cheviots.

We know that the brown-clothed lay brothers will be supervising these procedures. They are rather far from the tight control of the abbot at Newminster and there must be temptations to do a little hunting or to relax discipline. Some of the local landowners must have had trouble with them in the past. Although the landowners still seem to want to grant land to the abbey, at the same time there is a need for control. When Robert of Feritate adds land to that of the monks at Kidland, he specifies this in his charter:

> Praeterea saeculares conversantes apud Kidland fidelitatem facient abbati vel ejus assignato quod boscus meus et heredum meorum non dampnificetur per eos. Et conversi ibidem residentes hoc idem abbati in obedientiam promittent.

> Moreover the secular brothers at Kidland must act faithfully to the abbot or his assign who must thus ensure that the woods of me and my heirs are not damaged by them. And the lay brothers living there must promise the same obedience to the abbot. (p164)

Caistron and the Cospatrics

The Cospatrics were an ancient Northumbrian noble family with links back to the Anglo-Saxon king of England Ethelred II, to the kings of Scotland and possibly also to the kings of Ireland and Wessex.[88] They have a part to play in the history of Newminster because they made many grants to the abbey. Their charters are found in Gradus IIII. This is the area Rosie, Mary and I are now about to explore; around Caistron and the hamlets now known as Farnham and Wreighill near Hepple. Their family tree is in the appendix.

Ranulph de Merlay became connected with the Cospatrics when he married Juliana. Her grandfather, Cospatric I, had been made Earl of Northumberland shortly after the Norman

---

[88] Percy Hedley, pp 235 – 236

conquest in 1067. He was involved in revolts and wars against the conquerors, fleeing to his cousin the king of Scotland.

After series of political differences and battles, the family's fortunes changed when Cospatric son of Cospatric was granted the lordship of Beanley by Henry I at some date after 1100. This comprised Brandon, Beanley, Hedgeley, Shipley, Branton, Titlington, Harehope, Longhorsley, Stanton, Wingates, Learchild, Longwitton, Netherwitton and Ritton.[89]

Witton, Ritton, Wingates and Horsley were later transferred to Newminster.

We will remember too that Edgar, Juliana's brother, also signed a charter of agreement to her marriage. Edgar was a bit of a wild card. In 1138 he took the side of David king of Scotland, son of Malcolm III, and his second cousin.

In 1138 he had been part of a foray into the area around Hexham. We've referred to Richard Prior of Hexham who wrote about the depredations of the David's army into Northumberland. The prior uses some of his choice language for Edgar:

> At this time, certain lawless persons, whose sole study and delight was to plan and perpetrate crimes, banded themselves together in a detestable alliance … The chiefs of this abominable fraternity were Edgar, the illegitimate son of earl Cospatrick, and Robert and Uctred, sons of Meldred. Urged by rapacity and frenzied by passion, they overran Northumberland like wolves, seeking whom they might devour.[90]

What did Juliana think of her brother's activities and did Ranulph de Merlay find it an embarrassment? After all, it is possible that elements of David's army had damaged the monastery he had just established at Morpeth.

Perhaps Edgar settled down after he married Alice, the sister of Walter of Yvo, who among her marriage dowry brought manors in Coquetdale:

> … et in Cokedale, Tirwit et Cers, et Thosse et alteram Tosse et Flotweyton, cum nemore et plano et prato et cum aquis et molendinis … (p117-118)

> … and in Coquetdale, Trewitt and Caistron, and Tosson and the other Tosson and Flotterton, with its groves of trees and fields and meadows and with the waters and mills … (pp117-118)

Thirty pages of charters follow the first one in this section in Gradus VI in the cartulary. They detail the donations of the descendants of Edgar and Alice to the abbey. Those of Patrick son of Edgar come first, followed by John son of Patrick, and John son of John, and then another John son of John. It was one of the Johns who granted land to the Blessed John of Maidenley and Brother Hugh in 1247.

The earlier charters in this *gradus* must go back to the first decades of Newminster after 1138, not long after the time when Edgar was rampaging in Hexham. The family tree of the Cospatrics doesn't show a date for Patrick son of Edgar but it would seem logical that it would be around 1160.[91]

His first three charters are extremely generous. They list the rights to graze a certain number of animals on his pastures:

> Concessi quoque eis sufficientem pasturam in praedicta villa c matricibus ovibus et agnis earum usque ad Sanctum Michaelem, et x bobus ad terram suam colendam, et x vaccis et j tauro et vitulis earum donec superanentur, et v equis.

---

[89] Percy Hedley, p 236
[90] Prior Richard, pp 51 - 52
[91] Hedley, p 239

Also to them I have conceded enough pasture in the aforesaid village for 100 sheep and their lambs up to the feast of Saint Michael, and ten oxen living on the land, and ten cows and one bull and their calves until they are one year old, and five horses. (p119)

He makes available a pittance or special food allowance for a feast day:

… ad faciendam pitanciam conventui ejusdem loci annuatim in die Assumpcionis Beatae Mariae de aliquot pane et bona cervisia et salmone et aliquo pisce …

… for making of a pittance at the convent at the same place annually at the day of the Assumption of Blessed Mary of bread, good beer and salmon and other fish … (p118)

And he has a special request.

Et sciendam quod ego et uxor mea reddidimus nos et corpora nostra Deo et eis ut apud eos in morte nostra sepeliamur.

And notice that I and my wife will render ourselves and our bodies to God with them at our death to be buried at the abbey. (p119)

The abbot is very pleased with the generosity of Patrick son of Edgar. There follows a letter, rather than a charter, which he has sent to Patrick:

Concessimus quoque eis, ut in magno debito quod omni anno a capitulo Cisterciensi nobis injungitur, scilicet, ut unusquisque presbiterorum cantet xx missas et unusquisque clericorum x psalteria et unusquisque conversorum x p' specialiter. … et in missa cotidiana pro-patribus una collecta pro eis omni die usque in finem saeculi dicetur, et unum pauperem in infirmitoria saeculari pascemus pro eis in perpetuum; et ipsum Patricium et uxorem ejus recepimus ad sepulturam cum morientur, et faciemus plenarie pro eis servicia sicut pro ij monachis. Testibus, Johanne Priore, Eustacio suppriore, Gaufrido quondam abate, Gaufrido quondam abate de Salleia, Roberto cantore, etc.

We have conceded this to them, in the great debt that every year the Cistercian chapter charge thus that every single one of the priests will sing twenty masses and every single one of the clerics ten psalms and every single one of the lay brothers ten of the Lord's Prayer … and in daily mass a collection from them every day right to the end of time, and one pauper to be cared for in the infirmary for those outside the monastery; and we will receive Patrick and his wife to be buried after their death in our church, with the full service as provided for two monks. Testified, John the Prior, Eustace the under-prior, Gaufrid once abbot, Gaufrid once abbot of Salley, Robert the singer, etc. (p120)

One of the grants by John son of Patrick in the Caistron to Wreighill area mentions several boundary crosses in the description of the boundaries (p121). It is hard to work out where they were located because of the difference in place names between that time and this. But there is an unusual cross head in nearby Hepple church. David Dippie Dixon mentions that the cross was found on the moors near Paunchford by John Proudlock of Swindon, after which it was placed in the church.[92]

[92] Dixon, p 309

The nuns of Holystone

Much of this area where the Coquet river curves south and then east was dedicated to religious institutions; to the hermits of Caistron and the monks of Newminster; and at the same time on the other side of the river to the nunnery at Holystone.

Even more than Newminster, this convent is a faded and distant memory. Its origins are vague and its story obtuse. Rosie, Mary and I have passed through land they were granted at Nunriding about 18 miles from their home base.

The Newminster monks and their servants would certainly know about the nunnery as they came this way. They would be sure to encounter herders and peasants working for the nuns. Stories would circulate about these women who were enclosed but who perhaps came out and about at times.

We take a rest at the Lady's Well, a pool among a surround of shady trees. It has been a watering spot probably since the time of the Romans and is now a place of seclusion in the care of the National Trust. It may also have been the source of the drinking water for the nunnery as it still is for the village of Holystone. We are reading extracts of my photocopies from Dodds' history.

The original foundation of the nunnery is unclear. The great Norman de Umfravill family held Redesdale and land in the Coquet valley. They controlled this area from their castle at nearby Harbottle. It seems likely that either Robert de Umfravill, who died about 1145, or his heir Odinel I, was founder of the nunnery. The date is uncertain but it was possibly in existence at the time of Alexander, king of Scotland, who died in 1124. It certainly was there at the time of David I of Scotland, who reigned until 1153.

Dodds informs us that both Robert de Umfravill and Odinel were frequently at the court of King David. The nuns had received a large endowment of land in Roxburgh, where in 1213 it appeared that they founded a grange at a place called Hetun. There, they had agreement with the Helias, the rector of Old Roxburgh, in which they paid him three shillings annually from the tithes.[93] They also received rent from some land at Berwick.

We are aware how close we are to the southern borderlands of Scotland. In those days, there was ease of movement, and barons formed alliances with either country as it suited them.

---

[93] Madeleine Hope Dodds, p 460 and onwards, and Heritage Environment Record 1211

There are several surviving records of legal agreements made by the prioresses at Holystone. Diana, daughter of William Sellarius of Newcastle, had given them land at a place called Pandon. In 1230 Beatrix the prioress and her nuns leased this land to Robert of Valescyns at a rent of eight shillings a year with the consent of William, their master.

In 1240 Beatrix the prioress and the nuns made an agreement with the prior of Brinkburn, leasing from them some land in Caistron, just across the Coquet river for two pounds of cumin yearly. How did the nuns obtain this exotic spice? Trading networks must have extended this far into the countryside.

The Cospatrics donated land to the nuns of Holystone and the prior of Brinkburn, as well as to Newminster. By 1242 the nuns held 40 acres of land in Caistron rent free. In the same year they held land in Corsenside and Suttild in Redesdale from Gilbert de Umfravill and had income from Alwinton rectory. Over the hills to the north east, they were involved in land exchanges with Alice of Alnwick.

In 1255, when Henry III was at Newcastle, he confirmed the nuns in their possessions at both Holystone and Nunriding.

There was an agreement with the abbot of Newminster in 1272 to exchange 33 acres of land which the nuns held at nearby Flotterton with the same amount at Caistron held by the monastery. This was probably to consolidate the properties of each party.

A small nunnery it may have been, but its range was far and wide. As with Newminster, the century which preceded the war with Scotland seemed to be times of relative peace and development.

On 12th August 1296 the prioress Marjorie made a long overland journey to Berwick. Edward I demanded that Scottish nobles and clergy should do homage to him after his invasion of Scotland. She and her attendants would have to travel over the hills on a journey which probably took at least two days. It must have been intensely humiliating to have to bend the knee to this conquering monarch. The troubles of the nunnery were about to start. But as we sit by the Lady's Well in our white wool monks' outfits, Rose and Mary and I remind ourselves that for nearly two centuries the nuns of Holystone had managed land ranging from Roxburghshire to Redesdale, in Nunriding and Alnwick; all this as well as land and buildings on their own doorstep.

We go to see what we can find about the remains of the priory and the church. The little stream between Lady's Well and the village is bubbling along between its banks of marsh marigolds. All is bright and golden and green, and the sun is shining. But the strong wind is blowing big black clouds our way. I hardly need to say what happened next. We shelter in the church from the pouring rain for some hours, shivering and damp, thankfully drinking tea supplied by the hospitable parishioners for visitors and reading up on the documentation I've brought along.

There are few if any remains of the nunnery to be seen today, we learn. When the flocks and herds from Newminster passed through, there would have been a church, a cloister, a cemetery and domestic buildings. All have gone. Priory Farm across the road from the church may be built on the pattern of the original nunnery grange, and the present day cemetery to the north of the church is likely to be in its original location. Holystone village was the subject of one of the Northumberland National Park's village atlases where many more details can be found.[94] In the village, as with most monuments which existed at the time of Newminster and Holystone's best years, very little remains.

---

[94] The Archaeological Practice, Historical Village Atlas, Historical Synthesis, 2004, pp 374 - 375

In the 1100s and 1200s there was a Norman church here. This church was ruined in the early stages of the war with Scotland, and all hewn stones later removed to the rebuilding of the nearby Harbottle castle. It was not until 1848 that most of what was left of it was destroyed, and the church as we can now see it rebuilt.[95]

When the rain stopped sufficiently, we were able to see a few stones from the original church. In the west wall of the churchyard were some medieval fragments of carved stonework including a medieval gravestone. Three incised tomb slabs have been built into the south wall of the chancel. They are the merest of reminders of the passing lives of the nuns of Holystone and the world which the monks and shepherds passed through.

After Holystone the journey to the Cheviots is nearly over. The flocks would go on past the de Umfravill castle on its mound at Harbottle. And then on to Alwinton where there was a stone church built in the twelfth century, from which an original window still survives. That is a rare survival which we can be sure the shepherds and monks, and the nuns of Holystone, would have seen.

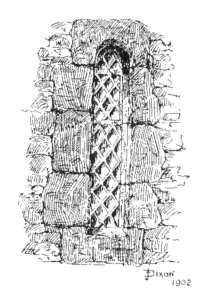

The 12th century window in Alwinton church

Shelter

We must think about where we are sleeping tonight. The wind is furious. The weather alternates between downpours and sunshine. We feel battered and worn out. Rosie's lack of a tent is a problem. We look at each other, none of us wanting to admit it. But when I wonder aloud if we might move to Clennell Hall a day early, Rosie's and Mary's faces lapsed into big smiles. Clennell Hall is the former hunting lodge, now a country guest house, where we had planned to stay once we arrived at the Cheviots.

In the open green grounds of the hall, on this Saturday night, are dozens of vans and boys and men dressed in tight black, red and yellow leather outfits, with motor bikes. Curious eyes look obliquely at three tired, bedraggled and damp female monk-like figures as we pass.

"Oh, I'm sorry. We are completely full," says the receptionist.

Our faces drop. "We can stay anywhere, in any little corner, even in the garage," we said. "We just can't face the wind and the rain again tonight."

---

[95] Madeleine Hope Dodds, p 455 - 458

Roz the manager looked at her young assistant. "Perhaps we could organise room nine and three quarters, the Harry Potter room?" she suggested. They moved out lots of stored items and found some mattresses and sheets. And that was where we were put, very thankfully, in a sort of junk room without a proper number.

As we lie cosily in our retreat we think about where the flocks and shepherds would have rested for the night on their way here from Newminster. We are now at the foot of the Kidland pastures. It would probably take them two days, with the night between, as it had us. The common pastures around Coltpark would be a good half-way point. There were watering places and fords once they reached the Coquet the next day. Tomorrow, we will look at where they stayed once they arrived in the hills.

Bridget, Mary and Rosie at Clennell Hall

6 In the green border hills

Seventeen thousand acres of hills and steep-sided valleys, rolling up and away to the vague watershed boundary between England and Scotland, empty except for sheep, shepherds and a few hikers and bikers. This was the land that, from 1181 until the wars with Scotland started with a vengeance in 1296, was the sheep and cattle ranch of the monks of Newminster; the land that fed the livestock in the summer.

Up from the lowland granges the processions came, animals in their hundreds, even thousands, with the accompanying carts and baggage ponies, guided by the shepherds and herders, the brown-robed lay brothers and their servants.

de Umfravill charters

It was the de Umfravill family who made available this 17,000 acres of land to the abbey of Newminster. They were the lords of Prudhoe in the Tyne Valley, but also of Redesdale, the wild upland river valley that stretches north westerly to the watershed of the Cheviots on what is now the border with Scotland near Carter Bar.

The de Umfravills were interlinked with the aristocracy of Scotland. The first of the family about whom a little is known is Robert. He was active in the 1130s. There is a suggestion that the de Umfravills obtained Redesdale from a Scots earl rather than a Norman king of England.[96] Robert regularly attended King David of Scotland.

His son Odinel had already granted land to Newminster at Filton and Tolland in the south eastern tracts of Redesdale. He died in 1156, so this was a very early charter tying in with the earliest days of the monastery:

> … Filton et quicquid ad eam pertinet, in bosco et in plano, in pratis, pascuis, aquis, molendinis …

> … Filton and all that pertains to it, in woodland and in plain, in meadow, pasture, waters, mills … (pp62-62)

The place names have changed but a hint from Hodgson has helped to locate them at Tone, on the A68 just north of Carrycoats.[97] This land was a considerable distance from the abbey. To get there the monks would have to follow the Wansbeck river to its source, and then go a little further. It seems likely that this land would also be used for upland summer grazing. Filton was later referred to as a grange (p65), and it survived as late as the dissolution. This and other charters are found in Gradus III of the cartulary. They include mention of Todholes, to this day a house on the steep hillside south of Elsdon, and Waterfalls, the modern farm near Sweethope Lough.

Thus, the idea of upland pastures remote from Newminster was already established by the time that Robert's grandson, Odinel II, gave the first grant of Kidlandlee to the monks of Newminster in 1181.

By then it was 43 years since the original foundation of Newminster. During this time, the importance of the wool trade to the Cistercian monasteries in England and Scotland was growing. The abbots of Newminster would be hungry for summer grazing grounds for their flocks. The same thing was happening just over the border in Scotland. Melrose Abbey had a grange at Hownam in the valley of Kale Water, and Kelso Abbey had a grange at Elliesheugh in the Bowmont valley.[98]

---

[96] Hedley, p 209
[97] Hodgson, Morpeth, p 50
[98] Hall, p 154 and 151

It made good business sense for the lords of Redesdale to have agreements with Newminster. There was so much wild, uncultivated hill land under their jurisdiction in Redesdale and Coquetdale that a rental income from the abbot would be useful, and at the same time good management might improve the land.

Thus Odinel II leased out the land, which is now more or less identical to the present forested area of Kidland, for 29 years. This is area 1 in the map which follows. The abbot had to pay the considerable sum of 220 marks for this, with a notional three more to Odinel's wife Alice and five to his eldest son Robert.

There were permissions and restrictions in the charter:

> … et de ipsa foresta ad omnia necessaria sua illius loci accipient, prout forestarii mei providerint, sine vastacione, et ita quod canes uno sui pede carebunt ut ferae meae indomitae pacem ibi habeant.

> … and from the forest they may take all that is necessary there which my forester allows, without ravaging, and that their dogs must have one foot cut off so that my wild game is left in peace. (p74)

Just as we saw in the earlier charters of the Bertrams, the de Umfravills were concerned to preserve their hunting rights.

This was the first of six substantial agreements which eventually totalled 17,000 acres. The boundary descriptions in the charters were carefully studied and applied to a map by the authors of *Drove Roads of Northumberland*.[99] The authors say that the boundaries are simply those considered most likely and that other interpretations are possible. They provide full details of the charters in their appendix.

Odinell II had four sons; Robert, William, Gilbert and Richard, the last who was his eventual heir.

After Odinell II's first grant of Kidland, William vastly increased the area for the monks with an agreement for land which went right up to the Scottish border, known by a variety of spellings but here I will call it Witetowes. The name could be linked with present day Trows Burn and The Trows, at the southern extremity of the granted area. This is area 2 in the map below. The exact date is unknown but it was before the date of William's death in 1195.[100] The rent was to be ten silver marks annually, five to be paid at the feast of Saint Cuthbert in Lent, and five in September.

The charter is long and detailed. Here are a few selections which show places familiar to present-day walkers in the Cheviots:

> … illam terram meas in Chiuittes moras quae vocatur Witetowes … et sic recte versus occidentem usque ad crucem quam praedicti monachi posuerunt per visum militum meorum ibi; … et per Wyndihege quantum ibi habeo usque ad ortum de Osweiburne … et per eundem rivum usque in viam de Hernespath …

> … all my land in the Cheviot moors called Witetowes … straight towards the west to the cross that the aforesaid monks put up there in the view of my knights … and from Windy Gyle as much as I have as far as the source of the Uswayburn … and by that same river as far as the road of Yarnspeth … (p75)

Yarnspeth is one of the old names for Clennell Street, one of the main historic routes into Scotland.

---

[99] Roberts, p 40 and Appendix 2
[100] Hedley, p 211

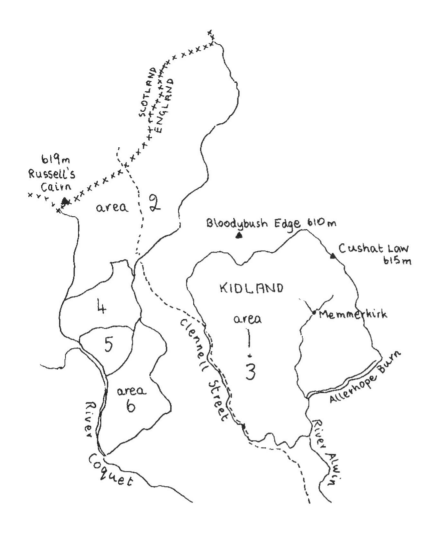

The six areas granted to the monks of Newminster by the de Umfravill family

Adapted from Drove Roads of Northumberland, by agreement

Richard was Odinell II's heir, and during his time as baron between 1195 and 1226 he made a succession of agreements with Newminster. One of them confirmed his father's original charter of 1181; thus areas 1 and 3 on the map are the same. It described the boundaries in much greater detail and affirmed an annual payment:

> ... annuatim iiij marcas argenti, scilicet, ij ad festum S. Cuthb. in xl^a, and ij ad idem festum in Septembri.

> ... four silver marks annually, namely, two at the feast of St Cuthbert in November and two at the feast in September. (p76)

He also agreed further land grants, shown as areas 4 and 5 on the map. They extended from William's charter in a southerly direction, following a steep-sided ridge of land bounded by the Trows Burn and the Coquet to the west, and the Uswayburn to the east. Area 4 included the names of Hepden Burn and Rowhope Burn. In area 5, Hepden Burn and Fairhaugh are named.

After Richard died in 1226, his son Gilbert inherited the land and he granted area 6 before his death in 1245. It is the hill now called Shillhope Law but was then called Turfill, or Turfhill, which we may assume indicates a source of fuel or roofing material for the abbey. The charter described a boundary by the Uswayburn to the lodge of William Bataille which is modern day Batailsheil.

In one of his charters, Gilbert confirmed all those previous charters from him and his ancestors. At the same time, he released the monks from ten and eight silver marks that they previously paid for their rents, and from all other demands that he and his family had made.

A memorandum followed this charter in the cartulary. It was a note written by one of the monks at the abbey:

> Memorandum quod iste Gilbertus receipit pro redditu xviij marcarum annui redditus clx libras, anno Dni. m°. cc^{mo}. septuagesimo.

> Memorandum that this Gilbert rendered eighteen marks annually totalling 160 pounds, 1270. (p80)

A parallel charter in the Filton section in this *gradus* also described this release from the rent:

> Gilbertus de Umfrauill comes Danegos, salutem. ... quietum clamasse ... redditum x et viij marcarum, quas dicti abbas et conventus solebant antecessoribus meis et mihi solvere annuatim, videlicet, pro grangia sua de Kideland viij marcas, et pro le Witetrowes cum pertinenciis x marcas. (p64)

> Gilbert de Umfravill, count of Angus, greetings. I quitclaim ... the render of ten and eight marks, that the aforesaid abbot and convent paid to my ancestors and to me annually, thus, for their grange of Kidland eight marks and for Witetrowes with its belongings ten marks. (p64)

This charter used the term *grange* for Kidland. It implied a farm; something more than a mere area of upland grazing.

A peopled landscape
In the period of the growth of Newminster's wool trade during the thirteenth century, this was a bustling landscape. There are traces of medieval villages, along the Coquet valley at Barrow, Linbriggs, Quickening Cote, Shillmoor, Passpeth and Gamelspath where Dere Street crosses the border.

There were travellers crossing the border via Clennell Street, The Street and many other routes. The monks from Kelso Abbey, or their servants, would pass through through Coquetdale into Redesdale to check the foals that they had been granted by the de Umfravills in Cottonshope.[101]

We have no description of the hill granges at Newminster and how they were tended by the people who lived there but we can at look at a study of one at Fountains and consider the similarities:

> The grange at Kilnsey in the Pennines was responsible to Fountains for sheep and wool. ... its description can be regarded as standard for other granges. The monks took over the hill farms in the area, and the tenants became shepherds for flocks put in their charge ... The accounts were kept under separate headings, such as the maintenance and feeding of sheep, repairing of boundary walls with hurdle fences, repairing of sheep houses and the washing and shearing of sheep, plus the transport and sale of the wool. At least two carters lived at Kilnsey, and regularly carried wool, butter and other produce the 25 miles to the abbey, returning with food. The valleys were cultivated and had meadows which provided hay, and rushes were grown for thatching ... one field was used to feed the lambs cows' milk in order to save the ewes' milk. The higher ground over 300 metres was criss-crossed with green roads, along which there are records of flock movements.[102]

There is a more recent description of what was life in the summer settlements in Scotland:

---

[101] Roberts, p 42
[102] M L Ryder, Sheep and Man, Duckworth, 1983 and 2007, p 450, citing Arthur Raistrick, *The Great Sheephouse at Malham*

It was the women who coped with this sojourn in the wilds. With them went girls who would help with the dairying, some boys to herd the livestock, and perhaps one or two of the elderly men.

At the shieling ground there were a few small dwellings, stone or turf-walled, thatched with heather. One would be kept for the dairying, where the milk and cream could stay cool. The living spaces were sparsely furnished, with some benches and stools, and perhaps a cupboard in a recess in one wall. Beds were of heather and turf laid on the floor, within wooden frames, with blankets for a cover. A fire would serve cooking purposes and provide warmth on chilly evenings.

On arrival at the shieling ground, the first thing to do, even before the main unpacking, was to milk the cows. This was a job that could not wait.   When the men who had accompanied the flitting had had something to eat and a good drink of fresh milk, they would set off back home and shieling life would begin. The cattle and goats would be put in the fold, a walled or wattle-fenced enclosure, while the horses might be tethered until they got accustomed to their new surroundings.

This description comes from Katherine Stewart's book *Cattle on a Thousand Hills.* It is a personal account dating back to nineteenth century Scotland, does not mention sheep, and is not from a monastic order. Thus it is not directly comparable. But it gives us an idea of the simple human and natural resources that were available. It emphasises that caring for the animals in the summering grounds was the work of women, girls, boys and elderly men. The strong adult men would go back to the farms where the heavy work of haymaking and harvesting needed to be done while the animals were out of the way.

Would Rosie, Mary and I find any traces on the ground of the activities of the flocks and herds, the shepherds and the lay brothers? After our first good night's sleep at Clennell we had a few days in which to investigate.

In Kidland forest
Areas 1 and 3 on the map are now covered by forestry. I am following the boundary described in Richard de Umfravill's charters, along the valley of Kidlandlee Burn upstream from its junction with the Alwin river. This day I am on my own, and I soon become immersed in forestry operations. The sound of sawing timber is filling the air. The landscape has totally changed from the grassy hills of the sheep ranges.

I walk along Clennell Street. On the way up, at NT 888 122, I am using my handheld GPS tool to locate what may be the west boundary of Kidland when held by the abbey of

Newminster.[103] I find a bank which fits the description, but if my find is correct it is endangered. Self seeded conifers of various ages are pushing their way through it.

From here I follow the boundary northwards around the edge of the forest. Leaving the trees onto the grassland I climb up Bloodybush Edge, a hill 610 metres high. Little white cloudberry flowers are growing among the peaty puddles and heather. From there the view down over Kidlandlee is like Northumberland's version of the destroyed Amazonian rainforests, sawn down trees and brown furrows with remains of roots sticking out. It is profoundly depressing.

The next day I go deep into the heart of the Kidland plantations. I follow the Alwin river, which is joined by the steep sided valleys of little burns, Allerhope Burn, White Burn, Meadow Sike and Sting Burn.

The Alwin valley, with Allerhope Burn coming in from the right. "Aller" means "alder", and "hope" means a small upland valley

Here I must quote how Kidland appears in a report by commissioners of the Crown in 1541, in which they describe the state of the borders:

> In summer seasons when good peace is between England and Scotland, the inhabitants of divers towns thereabouts repairs up with their cattle in summering as is aforesaid into the hopes and pastures of the said Kidland and so have used to do of long time.
>
> Kidland is full of little hills or mountains and between the said hills be divers valleys in which descend little rivvelles or brooks of water springing out of the said hills and all falling into a little river or brook called Kidland water which falleth into the river of Coquet near to the town of Alwinton within a mile of the castle of Harbottle. [104]

In 2013 the *little rivvelles* are descending between impenetrable banks of conifers. The air smells fresh and pine-scented; there is birdsong, and the sound of the bubbling water. But the *hopes and pastures* are empty of the voices of people, the barking of dogs and the bleating of lambs.

Medieval homesteads have been recorded here. In 1962 John Philipson placed them on a map showing their locations where the little burns, in their steep valleys, run into the river Alwin. They consisted of farm steadings and small enclosures for stock with traces of meadows in the valley.[105]

---

[103] Heritage Environment Record, Northumberland County Council, ID 512
[104] Bowes and Elleker, The Boundes and Meares of the Batable Land belonging to England and Scotland, 1550. Found in Hodgson, Part lll , vol ii, p222 - 224 notes, and excerpts in Dodds pp 450-451
[105] John Philipson, Sites on the Yokeburn, Archaeologia Aeliana 4th series, 41, 1962, p 61,

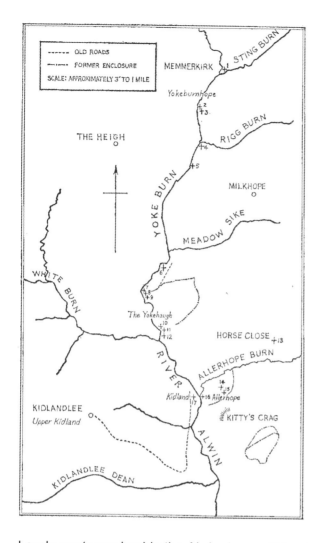

John Philipson's map of the Alwin valley, its tributary valleys and its homesteads marked with crosses

Map with thanks to the Society of Antiquaries of Newcastle upon Tyne

I cycle upstream beside the Alwin river until I arrive at Memmerkirk which is marked on John Philipson's map. This used to be thought a chapel belonging to the monks of Newminster. David Dippie Dixon, in his book 1903 book *Upper Coquetdale,* describes it:

> In the angle formed by the junction of the Yoke burn and Sting burn, at the southern base of Cushat Law, are to be seen ... the remains of Memmerkirk, supposed to have been a chapel erected for the use of the monks' servants when herding their flocks in the distant hill pastures of Kidland.[106]

Memmerkirk was excavated in 1962 by Barbara Harbottle and it proved not to be a chapel but a medieval longhouse.

> It seems reasonable to interpret the long house at Memmerkirk, with its associated enclosures, as a herdsman's shieling, perhaps built in the 15th century, abandoned no later than the early 16th century, and only occupied in the summer months.[107]

When I arrive there, Memmerkirk's site is overgrown with summer grasses and it is hard to make anything out. In an adjoining circular sheep stell some present day pilgrims have constructed a little shrine.

Another half mile up the winding track I arrive at a gap in the forest which allows a view up to Cushat Law, a round hill 615 metres in height. This hill is mentioned in Richard de Umfravill's boundary description as *Cousthotelau.* The roaring sound of great machines

---

[106] Dixon, p 42
[107] Barbara Harbottle, *An Excavation at Memmerkirk*, Archaeologia Aeliana 4th Series, Vol 41, 1962, pp 47 - 61

quarrying roadstone fills the air. The boundary goes on from Cushat Law to Sting Head, called *Steng* in the charter. There are boundary stones marked on the map there, but I don't try to approach the area. The motorcyclists at Clennell Hall had told us that they had been there on their trials the day before and that the area was all churned up, a mess of mud. Thus the world changes.

View up to Cushat Law, over cut-down forest and quarrying operations

The grassy sheep ranges

The other charter areas are mainly still open grassland. On the following day, now well rested, Rosie and Mary rejoin me and we set off on our exploration of the string of charter areas 2, 4, 5 and 6. In his book *Northumberland Landscape,* Robert Newton wrote this:

> In the wilds of thirteenth-century Upper Coquetdale the western limits of the grazing grounds of Newminster were defined by a stone bank and a ditch, which can still be seen. Beginning on the north bank of the river, opposite Windyhaugh, it ascends the grassy slope of Barrow Law, crosses the ridge … where a later drove road passes through the bank, through a gap marked by massive stones. This is sheep country of grass, bracken and scree.[108]

We find the bank and ditch and follow it up then down again to the gap through the massive stones. This boundary does not exactly tally with the map from the Drove Roads book. Still, it feels right.

Following the boundary bank and ditch up Barrow Law

The hill in the background is Shilhope Law, known as Turfhill, in the days of the Newminster monks

The bank runs from bottom left in the photograph as far as the stones, which leave a gap for the drove road to pass through

---

[108] Robert Newton, The Northumberland Landscape, Hodder & Stoughton, 1972, p 96

95

From here we follow paths as far as Windy Gyle, through areas 5 and 4. We climb the hill of Ward Law, from William de Umfravill's charter, and up as far as the border fence at Windy Gyle. At this point, we can see down into Scotland in the direction of the granges of Kelso and Melrose.

Rosie, Mary and I reach the shelter of the windbreak made of the stones of Russell's Cairn, a reminder of historic Border disputes which came later, to have our lunch. Hikers nowadays walk the Pennine Way here; this is a popular lunch stop. Most won't realise any connection with the monks of Newminster. Some of them look at us curiously. You don't often encounter monks on the Pennine Way, especially those of feminine contours.

From Windy Gyle, the boundary of the granted land heads off north-east. This is the highest area of William's charter. It is as though he is not precisely sure of his border here:

> et per Wyndihege quantum ibi habeo usque ad ortum de Osweiburne

> and from Windy Gyle as much as I have there as far as the source of the Uswayburn (p75)

This could be because it was still vague and unformed at this time, as the writers of *Drove Roads of Northumberland* suggest.[109] Or it could be that the area was so remote and it took such a long time to get there, that no-one perambulated it accurately and a little vagueness suited the purpose.

Perambulating the boundary between Scotland and England.

Along the border fence it is heathery and peaty, and rough pasture of minimal value for grazing. The white bobbles of cotton grass quiver in the wind. We head north easterly for a while before turning back into the Usway valley.

It is a long way across the upper grasslands to the green lower slopes. The places named in the charters are along the route, *Osweiburne, Ernespeth, Heppdenburne*. We reach the valley of the *Koket* and make our way back to our refuge at Clennell Hall. As we go, we are thinking and talking about the people who cared for the flocks, moving around here, during the great years of sheep rearing for the monastery.

---

[109] Roberts, p 40

Cheese and wool production

The work of the labouring people was essential to Newminster in its days of growing prosperity during the thirteenth century, when land acquisitions and rights of way agreements were continuing and the abbey church was being completed.

In his book *Sheep and Man* M L Ryder tells us a little about sheep rearing in the days of the Domesday survey, shortly after the Norman conquest:

> Milk was the main product of the sheep, wool and manure being by-products. The sheep would soon become primarily a wool producer which could be milked and folded to fertilise the land; meat remained unimportant.

> Sheep were found everywhere, and in greater numbers than all other livestock put together. Twelfth century stocking figures show that the sheep was increasing in numbers, but there is no indication which product was most important. Although the records refer to the large manorial estates, the livestock of the peasants probably equalled that of the manors in total numbers.

> Villeins on the Templar estates in Wiltshire had to send a woman to milk the sheep every day, and she received half the whey or half the buttermilk. A woman had also to be sent to wash the sheep, and then to shear them, at clipping time.[110]

Although this description refers to land in the south of England, there would be some parallels. Sheep milking, often the work of women, took place until recent times not far from here. In 2004, a survey on the Scottish side of the border found this:

> Buchts, or open-ended pens, used for milking sheep in the 17th and 18th centuries are common in the Southern Uplands. This survey has recorded 43 locations of at least 75 buchts. About half are single examples with the other locations having two or three. Some are close to shieling huts and other buildings.

> The shielings would have been used as temporary abodes during high summer when women and children stayed in them, tending flocks of sheep and some cattle, and keeping them away from the main farm where crops were exposed in the unenclosed fields. Shielings are less well known in the Southern Uplands than in the Highlands.[111]

We can picture the busy peasant families in their villages and on the hills in upper Coquetdale, who had to earn their food in a similar way from their small plots of land and livestock. If the ewes in the flocks from Newminster were milked, and this is likely particularly in the early days, then the milk products and cheese would have been a considerable source of wealth for the monks:

> Records show that the English medieval ewe produced between 7 and 12 gallons (32 to 54 litres) of milk during a lactation. According to Walter of Henley (an agricultural writer from the 13th century), twenty ewes gave as much milk as two cows, or enough to make four pints of butter a week and 250 round flat cheeses.[112]

It was the production of wool that earned Newminster its greatest wealth. There was a flourishing local operation involving clipping, washing, spinning, weaving and fulling for local use and sale. And there certainly was wool production for the international market.

One of the charters of Gilbert de Umfravill I, which we have not yet looked at, was an agreement with the monks for a fulling mill at a date during his time as baron between 1226 and 1245. This has received local fame in the last few years. The Coquetdale Community Archaeology group found the site of the mill in the Coquet river and excavated there during

---

[110] Ryder, pp 444 - 446
[111] Biggar Archaeology Report, Tam Ward, Upper Tweed Archaeological Survey, May 2004
[112] Ryder, p 448

the summers of 2011, 2012 and 2013. Gilbert de Umfravill's charter outlines its location which helped local people find it:

> Gilbertus de Umfrauill, salutem. … licenciam faciendi et firmandi stagnum molendini sui fullonici apud Hepden super terram meam ex australi parte de Coket, inter Hepdenburnemuth et Ruthopeburn …

> Gilbert de Umfravill, greetings … we licence the making and strengthening of a pond for their fulling mill at Hepden on my land from the south side of the Coquet, between Hepden Burn mouth and Rowhope Burn … (p78)

Commenting on this and the grange of Rowhope nearby, the writers of the *Drove Roads in Northumberland* say:

> From the Inquisition Post Mortem for Gilbert de Umfravill I in 1245, we learn that the monks of Newminster had another grange in Rowhope, adjacent to the Kidland pastures. Given the proximity of the fulling mill, which the Cistercians were permitted by Gilbert to build a little further down stream at Hepden (Barrowburn), it is tempting to see these installations as part of an integrated operation, with the fleeces from flocks shorn at the grange being processed at the fulling mill.[113]

Fulling is one of the final operations in the production of wool cloth. After the sheep were shorn the fleeces would be cleaned, followed by carding and spinning into yarn. Then the looms would come out. Long rolls of rather loosely woven cloth were produced which would still contain oil from the fleece. This was removed, and the cloth thickened, by the process of fulling. In earlier days the fabric was stamped or walked on, in tubs containing urine or fullers' earth. Later, water mills were used, where hammers stamped the cloth and after that process the cloth was hung out on great frames known as tenters.

All these processes were labour intensive. Shepherds, perhaps both men and women, would spin while watching the flocks. They would be weaving on the light summer evenings and at home during the long winters. Some of the wool produced at the fulling mill at Barrowburn would probably be used locally, including that for the monks' habits, while much of it would be taken by the carters to the abbey, to be sold at local markets. Sheep's wool was not always white, and there were grey, brown and black fleeces. The brown lay brothers' tunics could be woven from the natural colour of the wool.

But the most profitable part of the wool production was the sale of fleeces to the foreign merchants from Flanders and Italy.

How many sheep were there in the flocks from Newminster's granges, and what was the value of the trade to the abbey? These questions have been studied by David Jones and the Coquetdale Community Archaeology group as part of their research connected with the excavation of the fulling mill at Barrowburn:

> Unfortunately, there are no surviving Newminster records that tell us how large the abbey's flocks were, but we can get some idea of their size by looking at the abbey's export trade.

> Medieval Florence was home to some of the most skilled weavers in the world and around 1340 a merchant called Francesco Pegolotti documented the amounts of wool the city bought from various abbeys in the British Isles. The largest trade was done with the Yorkshire abbeys like Fountains and Rievaulx, who delivered 76 and 60 sacks of wool a year respectively. Newminster clocked in with a respectable 35 sacks. A sack was big, weighing in at 364 lbs, so this represented a shipment of 12740 lbs, or between 5½ and 6 tons. The fleece from a medieval northern sheep would have weighed less than 2 lbs, so this may represent the clip from between 7000 and 8000 animals.

> But Florence was not the only export market. Other good weavers were found in Flanders, and 65 years earlier, in 1275, Newminster had a dispute about a shipment of wool with a merchant

---

[113] Roberts, pp 40 – 41

from Douai called Jean Boinebroke. This shipment was over twice the size, weighing in at around 15 tons – perhaps the produce of some 20,000 sheep. The sack price of £7 tells us it was good quality wool (as it probably would be, given it was being exported) and the total shipment was deemed to be worth just under £650. With changes in labour rates, wages and inflation over nearly 750 years it's very hard to arrive at an accurate estimate of what this was actually worth, but even conservative calculations tell us that in today's terms this was a multi-million pound deal.

And, of course, that flock size of 20,000 is only a minimum. It doesn't include the sheep whose clip was sold to other merchants, or which was woven locally, so the real figure is probably higher. This was a lot of sheep, but we know that other religious houses kept flocks of 30,000 animals at around this time.[114]

Taking the wool to Newcastle

This source of wealth, the fleeces for foreign lands, had to be cleaned, packed and taken to Newcastle to the merchants' storage sheds ready for export. There are a few sources of evidence from the cartulary about the route they may have taken.

From the Cheviots, the carters would have had to take the paths and roads along the routes that Rosie, Mary and I had followed, back to the abbey and to its other granges like Horton. The fleeces had to be stored clean and dry so that they would not deteriorate and lose value. We don't know whether or not the fleeces were stored at the abbey as not enough has survived of the buildings. The arcaded cellarium or storage area in the west range at Fountains was used as a wool store.[115] It is possible there was a similar arrangement at Newminster, in the undercroft of the lay brothers' dormitory.

From Newminster, the fleeces had to be taken to the Tyne. The most obvious route was directly south from the abbey, avoiding Morpeth. The carts would head in the direction of the grange at Horton after crossing the bridge over the Blyth river, the rights to which had been granted by Roger de Merlay III.

Once past Horton grange, on the way to Newcastle, the abbey had obtained the right to pass through the village of Woolsington, roughly where Newcastle airport is now.

> Symon de Rue et Matild. uxor ejus, salutem. … conc. et praesenti scripto nostro conf. … liberum transitum … per omnes terras nostras villae de Wolsington …

> Simon de Rue and Matilda his wife, greetings. … we concede and this our writing confirms … free transit … through all our lands in the village of Woolsington … (p53)

Another charter granted rights of way through Fawdon and Kenton.

> Johannes filius Domini Roberti de Faudon, salutem. … conc. … liberam viam et passagium per omnes terras meas de Faudon et de Kynton, cum omnibus hominibus suis, una cum equis, carris, cariagiis, gregibus animalium et omnimodus averiis et necessariis suis, in latitudine xxx pedum …

> John son of Lord Robert of Fawdon, greetings. … I concede … free way and passage through all my lands of Fawdon and of Kenton, with all their men, with horses, carts, carriages, herds of animals and all the beasts and what is needed, for the width of thirty feet … (p34)

This route would bring the woolcarts in to the western fringe of Newcastle. There are a couple of hints confirming the route from a donor's charter in Gradus II:

> Riginaldus de Kynebell, salutem … conc. et conf. … liberum passagium et rivagium cum navi sua in terra mea de Edenstrem …

---

[114] David Jones, Coquetdale Community Archaeology, email to author, December 2013
[115] M L Ryder, p 450

> Reginald of Kynebell, greetings … I concede and confirm … free passage and landing place with their boats in my land of Eden Stream … (p52)

and

> … ad magnam viam quae vadit versus Trokeslau.

> … to the great road that comes through Throckley. (p52)

It is likely that Trokeslau means Throckley, in which case this indicates that the Newminster carts came to the Tyne on the western boundaries of Newcastle.

In Gradus II, there is also an agreement with a Newcastle townsman whose surname shows his Flemish origin. In this case the abbot has the right to bestow the licence on another body:

> … ita convenit inter Abb. et conv. Novi Mon. et una parte, et Gilbertum Flemyng, burgensem villae Novi Castri ex altera, … liberam licenciam faciendi quoddam stagnum ex transverso aquae de Derwent …

> … this agreement is between the Abbot and convent of Newminster on the one side, and Gilbert Fleming, burgher of Newcastle on the other … free licence to make a mill dam across the water of Derwent … (p52)

The Derwent joins the Tyne in the western edges of Newcastle.

Newcastle was a government-authorised staple town where merchants came to buy wool and the king's agents collected tax. T H Lloyd includes some details in his book *The English Wool Trade in the Middle Ages*:

> The Flemings … arranged that English monasteries from whom they obtained wool should themselves export it. Between June 1224 and July 1225 licences for shipping space to export it were granted to 16 abbeys, plus to the archbishops of Canterbury and York.[116]

Newminster is one of the 16 in the list which follows, along with the other well known abbeys such as Fountains and Furness.

It was all these activities in the hills and pastures, the production of food, cloth and fleeces for sale that maintained the life of two or three dozen monks at the abbey; the basis of what went on inside its cloistered walls.

---

[116] T H Lloyd, The English Wool Trade in the Middle Ages, Cambridge University Press, 1977, p 17

Pilgrims at Saint Robert's tomb, thirteenth century
Illustration by Victor Ambrus

7 The holiness of St Robert

Daily life

The Cistercian monks' day at Newminster, as at all their monasteries, consisted of three essential activities: praising God, spiritual reading and work.[117]

The first was the most time-consuming. The *Opus Dei* was the authorised form of worship. Eight times every day the monks attended the services, composed of psalms, the scriptures and prayer. The routine would vary according to the hours of daylight in winter and summer. Mass was said every day too.

The second was the *Lectio Divina*, the spiritual reading. Each day there was a meeting in the chapter house where any necessary business was discussed and a chapter of the Rule of St Benedict was read. Following this the monks would move into the cloister for their reading which lasted about two hours.

Third was work, the *Opus Manuum*, or manual labour. Depending on the time of year, it lasted between two and four hours. This took place in the afternoon, following the single main meal of the day which took place in the refectory.

These occupations were all to be completed between the rising and the setting of the sun. The manual labour was tempered to the skills and abilities of the individual monks. Necessary activities included gardening, field work and joinery, while younger monks might be occupied in copying manuscripts. Some of the work took place outside the cloister, in workshops or buildings in the outer close.

The lay brothers' routine was different. As we know, they performed more manual work than the choir monks and were often out in the granges. They attended fewer services and for those they used the western part of the church's nave, closer to the outer world.

Holy burials

The local nobility who made agreements with the abbey, or gave donations, often specified in their charters that they were to be buried in the abbey church. The questions arise: do we know if this actually happened as specified? And is there any evidence at the abbey today?

The *ancient roll* which is found after the charters in the Newminster cartulary gives some details of these burials:

> Et post mortem suam, praedictus Ranulphus, una cum Juliana uxore ejus, et Osberto filio ejus, sepulti sunt in boriali parte domus capituli illius monasterii quod condidit.

> And after his death, the aforesaid Ranulph, with his wife Juliana, and Osbert his son, are buried in the north part of the chapter house of that monastery which he founded. (pp267-270)

and

> Cumque Rogerus de Merlay … obdormivit in Domino, et in domo capituli Novi Monasterii cum patre suo sepultus est, et successit ei Rogerus filius ejus, qui dicitur Rogerus de Merlay secundus. … post obitum suum sepultus est in claustro ad introitum domus capituli …

> When Roger de Merlay … went to sleep in the Lord, and in the chapter house of Newminster was buried with his father, and his son Roger, who is called Roger de Merlay the second, succeeded him … after his death he was buried in the cloister at the entrance to the chapter house … (p271)

Thus three generations of de Merlays, Ranulph the founder, his son Roger I and grandson Roger II were all buried at the heart of the abbey.

---

[117] Summarised from the guidebook to Rievaulx Abbey, English Heritage, 2011, p 8

A later entry shows that Roger de Merlay III was buried there too, the fourth generation:

> … post obitum suum, sepultus est juxta Rogerum patrem suum, anno Domino millesimo …

> … after his death, was buried next to Roger his father, in the year one thousand … (p281)

Fowler observed, when he transcribed this, that in the margin of the *ancient roll* the date 1265 is written in a neat seventeenth century hand. This tallies well enough with Hodgson who noted that Roger de Merlay III died in 1266.[118]

It is probable that the four generations of the de Merlays were actually buried as the roll records. Each generation would know where their parents were buried.

We may remember too that Patrick, son of Edgar Cospatric, and his wife requested to be buried in the church, as stated in his charter granting land at Farnham. The grateful Prior John of Newminster confirmed his wish, with the full service as provided for two monks (p120). Thomas of Clennell too was assured by the abbot that he could be buried with the monks if he wished, and with the full service, just as for a monk (p163).

In the list of benefactors to the abbey, which is recorded in both Hodgson and as an appendix to the cartulary, there are more notes of influential burials in the church. Sir Ralph de Greystock in 1323 and Sir Robert Umfreville, Earl of Angus 1325, were both buried near the great altar. Sir Ralph, baron of Greystock, who died in 1374 is also listed as "buried in our church".[119]

There were plenty of human remains found in Barbara Harbottle's excavations of the 1960s, although no names can be attached to them. The presbytery, crossing and chapter house were the holiest places for burials, as close as possible to the heart of the abbey. In the presbytery, among the loose rubble, gravel and debris, human remains were found in the following trenches:[120]

In trench 12:

> Among this debris was found a skeleton wrapped in lead, which had obviously been moved from its original resting place and well shaken up, for the lead was holed and the bones disarranged.

In trench 14:

> East of the rubble, and covered only by topsoil, there were two grave covers, one above the other, and a small coffin. The upper of the grave covers was decorated with an incised cross and an illegible inscription, and the coffin, which was 4 feet long and made from a single stone, was partially covered by a piece of wood painted pink, and contained three skulls, sundry other bones and a lot of earth. It is clear from their positions and from accounts of earlier excavations that both grave covers and coffin had been discovered before.

In trench 15:

> South of the cobbles the sandy subsoil was overlaid by a thick level of brown clayey sand, in which were three stone coffins and a layer of hard mortar and stones covering a charnel pit. This contained a large quantity of human bones which, judging from their systematic arrangement, had been collected from other burial places in the abbey and deposited here.

There were human remains too found in the crossing and chapter house.

---

[118] Hodgson, Morpeth, p 11, notes
[119] Hodgson, Morpeth, p 52, and Appendix II Newminster Cartulary p 304
[120] Harbottle, pp 96 - 98

Eight skeletons in the crossing and chapter house were found associated with nails and strips of iron, the sole surviving trace of wooden coffins, and in some cases the nails still had wood adhering to them. These nails were some 2½ inches long, square in section and with flat circular heads.[121]

The three photographs which follow were all taken by Barbara Harbottle in the course of her excavations in 1961, 1962 and 1963.

Presbytery
Disturbed human bones, wrapped in a sheet of lead, re-deposited in the east end of the abbey church

Trench 12. Interpretation by Barry Mead

Photograph with thanks to the Society of Antiquaries of Newcastle upon Tyne

---

[121] Harbottle, p 168

Presbytery and monks' cemetery

A charnel pit containing a number of human skulls and other human bones. Probably the remains of earlier burials which had been disturbed by later grave cuts or building work and re-deposited here.

Trench 15 Interpretation by Barry Mead

South transept
An archaeologist carefully excavates human burials. The legs of the burial in the centre foreground have been covered by a jumble of other human bones including a skull.

Trench 17 Interpretation by Barry Mead

Photographs with thanks to the Society of Antiquaries of Newcastle upon Tyne

Another source of evidence for who might be buried at the abbey comes from a report on Newminster grave slabs. It appears in an article by archaeologist Peter Ryder in the publication *Archaeologia Aeliana* in 2002:[122]

> Excavations were carried out in the 1930s but were never properly published. Quite a number of cross slabs were found; some may have been re-buried, but others were removed into a museum in a hut or outbuilding. Their present whereabouts is unknown.

Among the twelve slabs which he described are two which bear lettering giving clues about names. The first was found in the north transept of the church. The person buried within has not been identified:

HIC : IA (CET) : (J)OHANNE(S) : ... ROYS : LORAIN : CVI : ANOIMA : REQIESCAT : I ;
PACE; SAME(N)

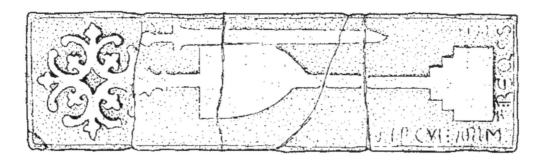

The second was identified as the grave slab of Joan Corbet, lady of Stanton. The slab alongside is assumed to be that of her husband, Sir Walter. He died around 1293; she about 1300.

HIC . IACET. DNA. DE. STANTON + JVANA CORBET

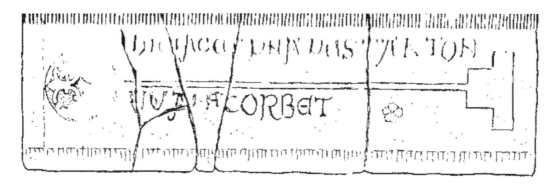

Drawings with thanks to artist Peter Ryder

In summary, although we know that the various donors of the charters expressed their wishes to be buried at the abbey, and human bones have been found there, there is no certain identifiable evidence. The remains are anonymous.

Charitable work

Newminster's cartulary has some charters which describe charitable work. This example is in an obit founded by Roger Maudut:

---

[122] Peter Ryder, Cross Slab Grave Covers in Newcastle and South East Northumberland, Archaeologia Aeliana, 5, XXX, 2002, pp 95 - 97

> Omnibus, Rogerus Maudut, salutem. … pro salute animae meae et animae Isabellae uxoris meae .. redditum xx s. per annum in molendino meo de Eschette … ad inveniend. tres pitancias honestas et competentes annuatim eisdem monachis in perpetuum … quicquid remanserit in praedictis tribus diebus detur portario ad portam, ut fideliter pauperibus distribuat pro animabus nostris.
>
> To all, Roger Maudut, greetings. … for the health of the souls of my and my wife Isabelle … the render of twenty shillings annually from my mill of Eshott … for providing three honest and decent pittances annually for the monks in perpetuity … and what remains after three days to be given by the porter at the door to the faithful poor for the health of our souls. (p17)

This and Roger Bertram's charter in an earlier chapter which refers to oatcakes and herrings are rare descriptions in the cartulary. This is not to say that the monks didn't do much more charitable work but rather that the cartulary is not the place where such records would necessarily be kept.

There is more evidence of their caring for the sick. There were many grants of land or income from land for the abbey's infirmary of seculars, which was a hospital for people from outside the monastery.

In Gradus IV there is a new *locus* which seems to be mainly about the infirmary. The locus is headed Ydyngton, which at first I took to be Edington near Morpeth. However it may be elsewhere. There are links in the charters with Tynemouth and two of them concern St Oswin. In the first, Hugh of Lakenby grants an acre of land for a candle to be burned *in praesencia Sancti Oswyni*, in the presence of St Oswin, and in the second this land is transferred to Newminster by Simon, Prior of Tynemouth.

Despite that uncertainty, this is clearly the *locus* where donations for the infirmary were stored together, and for reasons we cannot know it was a group of family and neighbours who supported it.

There are about thirteen of these grants, some seeming to be dedicated to keeping the infirmary light going, others mentioning only the infirmary, and others both. Here are some examples:

> Willelmus de Peggesword, salutem. … j rodam terrae cum suis pertin. in territoria de Ydington … ad inveniendum oleum in lampade infirmitorii saecularis ejusdem domus.
>
> William of Pegswood, greetings. … one rood of land with its belongings in the area of Edington … for the keeping of oil in the lamp of the infirmary of seculars at the abbey. (p171)

and

> Will. de Killyngword, greetings. … ij rodas et dim. terrae in meo territ. de Ydigton … specialiter ad sustenend. lampadem illam ardentem per noctem in infirmitorio saecularium coram Christi pauperibus ibi quiescentibus.
>
> William of Killingworth, greetings. … two roods and a half of land in my area of Edington … especially for the sustaining of the lamp to shine brightly through the night in the infirmary of seculars in front of Christ for the paupers sleeping there. (p172)

Hugh, Alan and William Lakenby have nine charters between them in this *locus.* William of Pegswood has three; and Robert Caluus has five. Women seem to have an influence here. William son of Cecilia of Edington makes six grants; and Robert son of Christiana Hasling also makes one grant of half an acre.

The life of St Robert
Over the decades, it seems probable that the abbey started to develop as a centre of pilgrimage based on the relics of Robert, the first abbot who was coming to be considered a saint. Such relics drew pilgrims who might receive cures and many would hope for some

relief from the future pains of purgatory. St Cuthbert's relics in Durham were a centuries-old draw, bringing constant streams of pilgrims and the associated wealth. Why should not the same thing happen at Newminster?

The two main sources of the life of St Robert which I'm using here are written in contrasting styles. First is from the *Oxford Dictionary of National Biography,* written by historian Henrietta Leyser, in a matter-of-fact style. According to his hagiographers, she writes, he was born in Craven, Yorkshire. Educated in Paris, he took up the rectorship of Gargrave before becoming a monk at Whitby and then part of the group that founded the abbey of Fountains. As we know, he was chosen to become the first abbot of Newminster where he arrived early in 1138.

Robert must have been an exceptionally energetic and well-organised person, as he oversaw the foundation of all three of Newminster's daughter houses within ten years, Pipewell in 1141-1143, Roche in 1147 and Sawley in 1148.

There were rumours which affected his reputation. He was on friendly terms with the hermit Godric of Finchale, who died 1170, and with the devout Edith of Hastings who lived nearby. Robert's name became associated with Edith, and to restore his reputation he visited his superior abbot, Bernard of Clairvaux, in France. Bernard cleared Robert's name and gave him a girdle which was subsequently revered among the relics at Newminster.

He was never formally canonized although miracles were recorded at his tomb. In 1656 the Cistercian order gave official approval to his cult.[123]

The second source is an article by Watkin Williams in the Catholic publication *Downside Review* of 1939 which expresses the story of St Robert in a reverent style. Williams based it on the version of the *Vita Sancti Roberti* edited by Pere Paul Grosjean in 1938 which originated from medieval sources. His article adds many details to our picture of the life of the monks of Newminster, including the apparent ease with which they moved around the countryside.[124]

Robert, he wrote, had been born in Yorkshire, probably between 1110 and 1120. As a young man, he showed signs of attraction to a religious life. He went to Paris, where he studied letters, philosophy and theology, and produced a work on the psalms, *Tractatus super Psalmos,* which has not survived:

> Here, (at Newminster) his *reverencia* and his *sanctitus* came to be held in such esteem that various magnates of the country-side, themselves providing sites, moved him to settle daughters of Newminster at Pipewell (Northants.) in 1143, at Roche (Yorks.) in 1147 and at Sawley (Yorks.) in 1148. An ardent lover of holy poverty, he would allow no superfluities, sometimes, as it might seem, even excluding necessities. Visiting the *conversi* (lay brothers) in the granges, he would ride some sorry beast of burden – no caparisoned palfrey, occupying himself in meditation and in the psalms, and avoiding the highways.

The article gives many examples of his saintliness. Once, when debilitated by hunger after a long fast, he accepted some buttered oatcake. Then instead of eating it he offered it to the first poor man at the abbey gate, who as the abbot knew was a messenger from heaven. At another time:

> … he was praying that he and his brethren, their service accepted, might find their names written in the book of life, when a voice from heaven assured him that only two of them had their names written upon earth.

---

[123] Oxford Dictionary of National Biography, Henrietta Leyser, Robert, abbot of Newminster, 2004-13
[124] Watkin Williams, Saint Robert of Newminster, Downside Review, 1939, pp 137 - 149

Making enquiries, he found that they were two lay brothers who had lapsed; not long afterwards they died a miserable death.

Some of the stories show that the abbot and his attendants, at least some of whom must have been monks, were not always confined within the cloister. In this encounter with the devil, Williams tells the story that Robert was passing through Newcastle when he saw an unusual person addressing a crowd.

> The Saint, realising promptly that this was no honest man's business, but the Devil's folly, told him in a commanding voice to break up the assembly without delay. 'Come along, my exquisite, you are not wanted by these people.' The man, thunderstruck, at once obeyed, and might be seen to leave his audience and make his way with dejected countenance along the streets and lanes in the footsteps of the Saint. The onlookers were amazed at the sight of an elegant coxcomb treading in the mud after a monk, tied, as it were, to his horse's tail.

When questioned this representative of the Devil revealed that he was working to inspire a riot at a wedding, in which the bridegroom would be slain, and "thus, many souls, their bodies dead, would fall to our lot".

Robert banished the Devil but the attendant monks were terrified by the incident, and their horses were controlled with difficulty.

Another story paints a picture again of activities outside the abbey.

> The monastery owned a little ship, navigated by two lay brothers and a few servants, used not only for the freight of necessaries but also for fishing. On one occasion, they suffered shipwreck and all their lives were lost.

At the time, Robert was saying Mass. After Mass, he assembled his community and told them about the shipwreck. He instructed two monks to go to Whitby where they would find the bodies on the shore under the cliff, and told them to give them due ecclesiastical burial. Ease of movement by the monks between Newminster and Whitby seems to have been taken for granted.

The story about the rumours is told in this manner by Williams:

> A noble lady and her husband, who inhabited a neighbouring castle, alas, unidentified, had been converted by him to such piety that in Lent they lived upon the food of monks and gave their delicacies to the poor. Delighted by their faith and devotion, St Robert would often visit the lady and seek to move her to yet greater spirituality. Evil suspicion arose in evil minds among the monks; neighbours and passing guests heard the story; at length it reached St Robert. … Aware of this … he took his way to Clairvaux to hear from the lips of St Bernard …

St Bernard cleared St Robert of the accusations:

> It was said that St Bernard bestowed upon the Abbot his girdle, which was … preserved among the relics of Newminster, being the means of restoring many sick folk.

This friendship between St Bernard and St Robert led to an introduction to Pope Eugenius III, who commended him to Bishop William of Durham, one of the consequences of which was a land grant to Newminster at Wolsingham in that county. (There are several charters in the cartulary relating to this land, pp45–47.)

The abbot was friendly with Blessed Godfric, the hermit of Finchal, a place on the River Wear about three miles from Durham. St Robert was Godfric's confessor, and when the abbot realised that his days were numbered he took his final farewell of Godfric. Soon afterwards, while praying in his cell, Godfric saw two angels bearing up the soul of the saint to heaven.

After much time, the body of the Saint was transferred from its original tomb and enshrined more honourably in the choir of the abbey church; and that of some of the many miracles wrought at both places we are not to hear. The date of this translation is unknown.

Williams recounts several of the miracle stories. A thief was restored to honesty; a man was cured of insanity; a man who had suffered fever for years was cured; a monk who fell from a ladder while painting the dormitory called upon the saint's name and was gently placed on his side when he fell; two monks and two youths found themselves in danger of being crushed by an ox-team on a steep hill slope, when they called upon the saint and the wagon stopped.

There is a new translation of the *Vita Sancti Roberti*. In it are a few more details about the tomb of Saint Robert:

Now the holy father crossed, rich in merits and clear in miracles, from the world to the Father in the year of the incarnation of the Lord 1159 the 7th of June, and the most holy corpse was placed in a stone memorial, on which grand marble and precious jewels had been placed.

and

... at first in the chapter of that monastery, but after a long time, with the body having been transported into the church, it is now held in the monastery more honourably.[125]

Robert died on 7 June 1159. His feast is still celebrated on this date by Catholics in Morpeth, Newcastle and beyond.

Lights at the tomb
As we know, most of the original charters for Newminster were from the important local families. In return for their donations they could receive the prayers of the monks for the salvation of themselves and their families, and even burial at the monastery. But there was a way in which people of lower social status could show their piety and share in the benefits to their eternal souls. This was by the provision of lights:

Whilst donors or grantors of high social status had a range of strategies for salvation – place of burial, (con)fraternity, chantry, pittances in expectation of response – the exchange of rents for lights in expectation of salvation was much more accessible to lesser benefactors.[126]

and

Lights are significant because quite modest endowments could be made for their maintenance, which allowed the participation of wide social groups in this form of association with the liturgy, including burgesses and even the free peasantry.[127]

We have already seen charters for the provision of lights to the infirmary of seculars. Newminster's cartulary also contains a particularly interesting group of charters concerning lights at St Robert's tomb. Before looking at them, here is an extract from a single one tucked into Hodgson's *History of Morpeth* and which he translated. It is dated 1267:

John de Plessey appropriated five marks sterling to be paid annually to the abbot and convent of Newminster and their successors, for ever; half at the feast of St Cuthbert in March and half at the feast of the same saint, in September, for the purpose of finding two waxlights of two marks value, by the keeper of the light around the tomb of St. Robert, the first abbot of Newminster; which wax-lights should be lighted, and burn in the way and order in which the other four lights were found there for him ... out of the mill of Stannington.

---

[125] Translated by Linsey Hunter, Chapters 9 and 10, pp 355 - 356
[126] David Postles, Lamps, lights and layfolk: 'popular' devotion before the Black Death, Journal of Medieval History, Vol 25, no 2, p 105
[127] Postles, p 98

Also the same keeper was to provide the same convent, on the day of the Deposition of St Robert, such things to eat and drink as were proper and sufficient; and the remaining three marks be directed to be specially given to the said convent, by way of addition to two marks which he had before given them as pittances, out of the mill of Stannington, so that 20s. should be spent at his own obit, one mark at his mother's, 10s. at the obit of sir Richard his father, ten at that of the lady Idonea his mother, half a mark on the anniversary of sir Roger de Toggesdene, and another half mark at that of the lady Agnes, wife of the same Roger.[128]

If we move now to the Newminster cartulary, we have clear evidence that the people of Morpeth and the surrounding area were drawn by the holiness of St Robert's tomb. The first sign of it appears in Gradus VI:

Willelmus Butler aeternum in Domino salutem … specialiter ad luminare Beati Roberti, primi abbatis ejusdem loci imperpetuum, unum toftum et croftum et xxx acreas terrae in villa et territorio de Nova Pendemore …

William Butler greets you in God eternal … especially for the lights of the Blessed Robert, first abbot of the same place in perpertuity, a toft and croft and 30 acres of land in the vill and territory of Nova Pendemore … (p225)

This charter is not dated, and at the time of writing I have not identified Nova Pendemore. However it is in a section of the cartulary which includes confirmations of land by Roger Bertram of Bothal. One of them has the date of 1282, so there is a probability that the charter is from a similar time and place.

In Gradus VI, among the many land grants are ten which specifically provide income for lights at the tomb of Saint Robert. This is in the Tritlington and Earsdon section. The sums of money are sometimes quite small and women feature in them frequently. Here are some selections:

Dyonisia quondam uxor Fulconis de Tybenham, salutem. … specialiter ad luminare Beati Roberti, unam acram terrae in territorio de Tyrtlyngton …

Dyonisia, sometime wife of Fulconis of Tybenham, greetings. … especially for the light of the Blessed Robert, one acre of land in Tritlington … (p230)

and

Robertus Stilche et Margareta uxor ejus, filia Eustachii de Erdisdon, salutem. … specialiter ad luminare B. Roberti primi abbatis ejusdem loci, … unam acr. terrae cum suis pertin. …

Robert Stilche and Margaret his wife, daughter of Eustace of Earsdon, greetings. … especially for the light of Blessed Robert the first abbot at this place, … one acre of land with its belongings … (p232)

After page 232, the area from which the grants are coming changes:

Robertus Merwyn de Meldun, salutem in Domino sempiternam. … luminari beati Roberti primi abbatis Novi Mon. pro me et her. m. imperpetuum, sex den. annuatim redditus … custodi luminaris praenominati qui pro tempore fuerit, fideliter respondeat.

Robert Merwyn of Meldon, greetings in the Lord eternal. … for the light of blessed Robert the first abbot of Newminster for me and my heirs in perpetuity, six pence rendered annually … for the named custodian of the lights whoever he may be at the time, may he answer faithfully. (p234)

and

---

[128] Hodgson, Morpeth, p 52, and History of Northumberland Part III ii, the Latin version, pp 73 - 74

Christiana de Mithford, salutem in Domino. ... luminari Beati Roberti de Novo Mon. sex denarios annui redditus recipiend ...

Christiana of Mitford, greetings in the Lord. ... for the lights of Blessed Robert of Newminster six pence rendered annually ... (p236)

and

Ricardus Ters de Morpeht, aeternam in Domino salutem. ... et specialiter luminari Sancti Roberti primi abbatis ejusdem domus in redditum duodecim denar. argenti annuatim ...

Richard Ters of Morpeth, greetings in the Lord eternal. ... and especially for the lights of Saint Robert the first abbot of the same house, rendered twelve silver pence annually ... (p237)

Other donations include one half of a toft in Earsdon from Ranulph of Tritlington, five silver shillings from Robert of Lynemouth, one acre of land from Henry of Earsdon and forty silver pence from William Faber;

After all these pious donations comes a most significant charter and the only one of this type that I have seen in the cartulary. We will remember that in the Cistercian system each daughter abbey received a visit every year from its mother abbey. Thus the abbot of Fountains visited Newminster annually, just as the abbot of Newminster visited Roche, Pipewell and Sawley.

One day in March 1274 Brother Reginald, the Abbot of Fountains, visited Newminster in the company of Geruasio, the abbot of Holm Cultram in Cumbria. There, he signed a document which is able to demonstrate to us an important developing pilgrimage site at the tomb of St Robert. The Latin version is provided in the appendix. Here is the full translation, made especially for this book:[129]

Brother Reginald, said abbot of Fountains, to the sons of the new monastery chosen in Christ both now and to come everlasting blessing in the Lord and complete perseverance in the sacred (task) proposed.

Concerning the revering with greater devotion and more ceremony of the memory of your most blessed father Robert, under your negotiating care and hard work, the pious devotion of the faithful is known to have collected a payment of six marks. This deservedly encourages and urges your minds especially and particularly, as not ignoble sons, to love more sweetly, honour more closely and imitate more firmly the saint himself.

We too, wishing to stir your minds to the honour and glory of Almighty God and the Blessed Virgin, and the very holy father himself, want, allow and decree with regard to your petition and that of your Lord abbot, (consulting too for this matter Lord Gerausius, the venerable abbot of Holm then who was present) that for collecting the said payment of six marks, and in the same way spending what is mentioned below, in perpetuity, someone among you, farsighted and especially prudent, should be appointed to provide from the revenues of the aforesaid payment eight candles annually as is the custom around the tomb of Blessed Robert.

And besides, on the day of the anniversary of the death of the same father, from the remainder, as far as it can be stretched, the interest of the aforesaid income will obtain for your monastery food in plenty.

But this arrangement of yours which has been set down, we want, decree and give instructions under the virtue of obedience both by you and your successors in perpetuity to be observed inviolably and unalterably, on the authority of God and our rule very carefully preventing anyone of you or your successors to go against this deed to any extent at all, or to transfer in any way the said income to other uses apart from what has been set down.

---

[129] Translated by Teresa Saunders

Also, for this reason, so that all these things written above may continue in perpetuity, I, brother R, abbot of Fountains, Lord G, abbot of Holm and Lord Adam, your own father, have put our seals to this writing as evidence and confirmation.

Given at the New Monastery, in the 1274th year of grace, on the next day of March after the Ascension of the Lord. The convent of the same house is witness. (p237)

This lengthy document is doing several things. It is approving the sacred task of honouring the memory of St Robert at his tomb. It congratulates the care and hard work of the abbot and the devotion of the faithful in collecting the six marks. It endorses the appointment of a special person to care for the tomb and the purchase of eight candles annually which must stay lit. At the same time, the anniversary of the death of St Robert is to be marked with a splendid feast at the monastery.

A warning follows against any use of this money for other purposes. The authority of the seals of the parent abbot of Fountains, and those of the abbots of Holm Cultram and of Newminster too, lends full weight to this serious document. The final sentence implies that all the monks were witnesses to the original signing, so this visit must have been a memorable event.

By establishing this letter fully in the minds of all present, and by endorsing the donations of the members of the community outside, it seems clear that the lighting of the tomb and the ritual at the feast of St Robert is being established. Pilgrims will be drawn to Newminster. They would have made their way from Morpeth, crossing the Wansbeck, and circling around to the west entrance into the church. Some of them may have stayed at the *spital* of St Leonard, near Mitford. It seems that by this time women too must have been allowed into the church, if not into the inner cloisters.

There are parallel stories in other Cistercian monasteries. At Rievaulx, William the first abbot came to be considered a saint. At Melrose too, Waltheof, one of the earliest abbots and stepson of King David I, was honoured in the same way.

These developments were happening without any knowledge of the problems which were soon to follow. Two short decades later, the pivotal year of 1296 arrived. Edward I took his army into Scotland, crushed Berwick and quickly subdued the borderlands.

The golden years of Newminster would become eclipsed. After this time the armies of the kings of England, on their way back and forth along one of the main routes between the two nations, would frequently use the facilities of the abbey. There was ravaging and destruction by the Scots, while the English did the same over the border. The difficult days for Newminster were about to begin.

Left, the seal of Fountains Abbey
Right, the seal of Newminster Abbey

114

8 Difficult days

The charters suddenly stop

Newminster was hugely disadvantaged by the wars between Scotland and England. For more than two centuries after Edward I's invasion and crushing of Berwick in 1296, armies and groups of raiders from both sides passed back and forth over the county. Richard Lomas provides useful background information:

> Warfare lasted on and off for over three hundred years ... but it was by no means continuous. In the fifty years between 1296 and the battle of Neville's Cross in 1346 a campaign of some sort took place in one direction or the other almost every year. Thereafter, however, bouts of fighting were short, lasting a few months or at most a few years, and were separated by periods of peace, or more accurately truce, of up to twenty years.

There were two other damaging factors:

> The severe famine consequent on a sequence of three disastrous harvests between 1315 and 1317, and the reduction of flocks and herds in the subsequent years to 1322 were calamities from which the North East was not excepted. More damaging in the long run was the Black Death of 1349, which may have killed about half of the region's population.[130]

These events didn't stop things entirely. We know from Pegolotti's list that the wool sales continued into the 1300s but the days of expansion are over. If we refer back to the pigeonhole diagram we can see that the change is immediate.

From early in the reign of Edward I, who came to the throne in 1272, charters began to be dated. In the Newminster cartulary, in the period between Edward's accession and his invasion of Scotland, there are three showing dates: in 1272 there was an exchange of land between Newminster and the nuns of Holystone (p141); in 1292 John of Swinburn released all claims to the abbot from his manor at Filton (p68); and in 1296 there was an agreement with the rector of Rothbury about tithes (p143).

After 1296 the charters become few and far between.

In the early decades of the 1300s there is a small cluster in Gradus II, and they relate directly to war damage. This one from 1315 is a clear statement from Bishop Richard Kellaw:

> Ricardus episcopus Dunelm, salutem. Considerantes dampna, jacturas, et oppressiones quae dilecti nobis in Christo Johannes abbas Nov Mon. et ejusdem loci conventus per crebras invasiones et devastaciones Scottorum sustinuerunt, et ad instanciam illustris domini regis Edvardi Angliae, quantum in nobis est, concessimus ... et confirmamus quod iidem abbas et conventus et eorum successores habeant et teneant manerium suum de Cheppwell in separali ... suo omni tempore anni in perpetuum ...

> Richard bishop of Durham, greetings. In consideration of the damage, the losses and seizures that our dear brother in Christ, John abbot of Newminster, and all his convent have sustained through repeated invasions and devastations by the Scots, and at the instance of our illustrious King Edward of England, as far as is in our power, we concede ... and confirm that the abbot and the convent and their successors should have and hold his manor of Chopwell in perpetuity ... (pp48-49)

Two more charters shortly after this release the abbey from all rents and services on lands in Chopwell, one from Robert de Umfravill and the other from John, son of Richard of Horsley. They look as if they are a way to help the abbey in its time of need. They are dated 1317 and 1313 (pp 50 – 51).

---

[130] Richard Lomas, North East England in the Middle Ages, John Donald, 1992, p 54

It is not until the 1400s that new clusters of charters appear, mainly in Gradus V, VI and VII. In Gradus V, there are many between 1424 and 1489 and in Gradus VI, between 1416 and 1487. These include the cluster of grants for lights at the tomb of St Robert and leases for booths at Newcastle market. However not all the charters in these *gradus* are from this time. As we've learned before, donors and places took precedence over chronology in the cartulary.

To find out more about what happened to Newminster after 1296 we need to branch out beyond the information provided in the cartulary.

Kings and armies at the abbey

Morpeth, and hence Newminster, is on two of the main routes into Scotland. The two roads separate just north of the town, one to Berwick and one to Coldstream. The abbey provided a convenient stopping place for the kings and their armies, and its duty of hospitality put a huge strain on resources. In his introduction to the cartulary, Fowler puts it like this:

> The frequent friendly resort to them, also, of the royal army, and of noblemen and others, both from England and Scotland, was represented as exceedingly burdensome.[131]

Hodgson has a few records from this period in his *annals*:

> On Sept 29, and Oct. 1, in this year, 1296, Edward the First, as he returned from the conquest of Scotland with the inauguration chair of the kings of that country, tested different public documents at Morpeth.

and

> In 1301, Edward the First was at Morpeth on June 28, on his march with the second division of his army into Scotland ... [132]

Fowler lists Edward II as dating public documents at Newminster in September 1310; on September 8, 10 and 11, 1311; and on May 30 and from June 4 to 7, 1314. This is a total of four times in four years, surely a considerable burden on abbey finances. Edward III visited on November 16, 1334.[133]

After 1296 details of the effect of Scottish invasions on Newminster are hard to find anywhere. I've had to turn to specialist historians:

C J McNamee has written about William Wallace's incursions into Northumberland in an article in Northern History Review.[134] In response to Edward's invasion of Scotland, William Wallace defeated the English army at the Battle of Stirling in September 1297. After that, he and his army rampaged through Northumberland. Nothing on this scale had happened before. The people of the county were terrorised:

> At that time, the praise of God ceased in all the monasteries and churches of the whole province from Newcastle to Carlisle. All the monks, canons regular and the rest of the priests and ministers of the Lord, together with almost the whole of the people fled from the face of the Scot.[135]

As far as Newminster and Morpeth were concerned, the initial appearance of Wallace's invasion was of scattered bands of marauders who came very close. By October a camp was established in Rothbury Forest, from which the Scots raided the surrounding countryside, and a mill at Felton, only eight miles north of Morpeth, was burned around the 13th of that month.

---

[131] Fowler, p xii
[132] Hodgson, Morpeth, pp 122 - 123
[133] Fowler, p xii
[134] C J Namee, William Wallace's Invasion of Northern England in 1297, Northern History Review, 1990, pp 40 - 58
[135] The Chronicle of Walter of Guisborough, cited by C J Namee , p 40

Burnings took place in the north-east corner of the county, at Norhamshire and Islandshire, Lowick and Bowsden, Embleton and Ellingham. Longhorsley parish church was destroyed, and destruction was particularly heavy around the Cheviot, at Yeavering, Hedgely, Hepburn and Doddington. All over the countryside people fled to walled towns and castles. Alnwick castle was able to send out troops to harrass the raiders but was not able to prevent the town being fired.

At some stage in November the army of Scotland moved south, scattering the tenantry. Woodhorn on the coast seems to have been abandoned, as was Stamfordham. After bypassing Newcastle, Wallace went on to wreak havoc at Bywell and Corbridge, before arriving at Hexham.

These events were so close to Newminster and Morpeth that the fear and trembling must have been general but there is no specific reference to these places. The closest Wallace's army seems to have come is after it returned from savaging Cumberland. On 18 November 1297 they passed Hexham and the Tyne valley, avoiding Newcastle before heading north for home. On the way they attacked Mitford castle on 25 November, burning all the corn in the grange.

McNamee draws attention to *A Song on the Scottish War*, a contemporary description written by a prior of Alnwick, and here we find a reference to Newminster. The prior laments how the town of Alnwick was put into flames. We then find this:

> Many ask each other how it happened
> That the Newminster was not touched by the fire.
> The monks promise gifts,
> But they do not fulfil their promise:
> As there was need, so was the thing carried into effect.
> On this account they led away captive the prior of the monastery,
> Whom they then found.[136]

Thus although Morpeth and Newminster were in the path of Wallace's army both on its journey south and its return northwards, and many very close neighbouring villages and buildings suffered, the abbey buildings seem not to have been damaged and neither, it seems, was Morpeth. What happened to the poor prior who was taken hostage we don't know.

Although the abbey avoided damage, it is certain that its holdings in the countryside were badly affected. The ravagings of Wallace were followed by those of Robert I of Scotland, better known as Robert Bruce. In the words of Richard Lomas, these were the darkest and most miserable conditions Northumberland has ever had to endure.

> How bad did conditions become? A precise and completely accurate answer is not possible since the evidence is so limited, and in some cases to be suspected of exaggeration. This is particularly so of the petitions submitted to the Crown by monasteries. Admittedly as static and pacific institutions they were particularly vulnerable, but they were staffed by literate and educated men who were well versed in making a good case to their own advantage.[137]

Lomas makes it clear that it was during the time of the "idle and incompetent" English king, Edward II (1307 – 1327), that the North East was open to Scottish depredations.[138] It was between 1311 and 1329 that the Scots had the upper hand. Robert Bruce had considerable military and political abilities, and took advantage of Edward II's incompetence.

---

[136] Thomas Wright ed, The Political Songs of England, 1832, republished 1996, ed Peter Coss, CUP, pp 173/174
[137] Lomas, County of Conflict, p 40
[138] Lomas, North East England in the Middle Ages, pp 54 - 55

In 1311 he began large-scale raids into northern England, with more again between 1315 and 1322.

An article by historian Jean Scammell explains the system of blackmailing and terror imposed by his armies on Northumberland and through the county of Durham as far as the Tees. Only people who could retreat into their fortresses had any chance of survival, and there were many refugees with their animals. There is one brief mention of a payment to the Scots by the Abbot of Newminster for his manor of Chopwell in 1318. She writes that the monks needed an augmentation of their income "because of the burden of hospitality to magnates, both Scots and English".[139] This statement leaves us with the idea that the pacific monks were obliged to play host to whichever powerful group arrived at its gates.

Edward II certainly stayed at Newminster, as Fowler reported, in 1310, 1311 and 1314.[140]

Northumberland's long years of agony were brought to an end in 1329 when Robert Bruce died, probably of leprosy. In the same year, Edward III re-took the initiative. In July 1333 the Scots were routed at Halidon Hill, north of Berwick, by his army. While he was in the north, as Fowler reported, Edward III "tested a mandate" at Newminster on 16 November 1334.[141] Northumberland had survived and would come back to life.[142]

Border conflicts continued over the next two hundred years. It is curious that Hodgson's record of Morpeth's annals of the fourteenth century calmly lists a series of land transactions, with not a mention of the upheavals.[143] Nevertheless the plunderings must certainly have affected Newminster's tenancies across the countryside and greatly reduced its income.

New sources of income

New sources of money were needed to keep the abbey going. One of the ways to do this was by obtaining income from churches and, in Newminster's case, although Cistercians had not originally been allowed to accept unearned income, *advowsons* at the churches of Stannington and Kirkwhelpington were obtained by the abbey. In case of need the rules were being more flexibly interpreted.

An *advowson* is the right to control who should be the rector of the church. The holder is in the position of obtaining much of the income from tithes.

The records are few but the advowson at Stannington is referred to in the list of benefactors in the appendix to the cartulary (p302). It is also translated into English by Hodgson:

> Roger de Somerville, who gave to us the advowson of the church of Stannington, died Jan. 18, 1335, and was buried at Burton Agnes.[144]

The source for the income from Kirkwhelpington in Tynedale ward is from Hodgson again:

> Edward the Third granted 23rd October 1334, a licence to Gilbert de Umfravill, earl of Angus, to sell the perpetual advowson of it to the abbot and convent of Newminster, and to have it appropriated to their own proper use.[145]

Hodgson reports on the wording of the monks' petition:

---

[139] Jean Scammell, Robert I and the North of England, English Historical Review, July 1958, pp 385 - 403
[140] Fowler, p xiii
[141] Fowler, p xiii
[142] Lomas, p 44
[143] Hodgson, Morpeth, pp 115 - 163
[144] Hodgson, Morpeth, p 51
[145] Hodgson, Part II i, p 204

It describes their house as laid in ashes; their lands wasted by the frequent inroads of the Scots; and their tenantry so spent and weakened by pestilence and contagious diseases, that they were unable either to maintain their household, to repair their dilapidated buildings, to bestow their customary alms, or to support the great influx of nobility, and others, who resorted to them for hospitality.[146]

The raising of income from property seems to be becoming a normal source of income for the monks. Hodgson relates various examples:[147]

Edward the Third, Oct. 1, 1343, recites letters patent of his father licensing the abbot and convent of Newminster to acquire in fee, lands or rents, to the value of £50 a year.

This seems to be a confirmation of the right to take income. It is followed by a list of properties in Morpeth and other areas. The rents total to "about three score and sixteen shillings and sixpence a year".

Hodgson records two further documents, dated 1364 and 1392, during the reigns of Edward III and Richard II. The first empowers the abbey to acquire lands of named people in Morpeth, Stannington, Thornton, Wotton, Idryngton, Aldworth, Pendemore and Corbridge, totalling £8.4.2d per year. In the second, in consideration of £10 paid to him by the abbot, Richard II licenses Newminster to receive seven messuages of land in Morpeth and six in Newcastle, as well as rent of 4 shillings from a close beside Close-gate and three acres of ground.

In another, Ralph, baron of Greystoke in 1389 grants to Newminster the income from 14 lands and tenements in Morpeth when they fall to him on the death of his mother.

The abbey is clearly building up a portfolio of rental properties.

There are a few more donations listed by Hodgson in this section of his *History of Morpeth*. What makes them different from the charters in the cartulary is that the rent is a source of inward income to the abbey. Earlier, the abbey sometimes paid out rent, or was released from rent and other obligations by the donor. The time of the monks and their lay brothers managing the granges as the abbey's main source of income has ended.

Newminster's properties in Morpeth

We might wonder what impact the monks had on life in Morpeth as the years went on. Some indications of properties they held in the town can be found in Hodgson again.

Morpeth's annals, which are the events worthy of recording as far as the burgesses were concerned, are nearly all to do with land transactions. Because maps were not used in the early days, boundaries are described as with the charters, and many of them mention properties held by the monks.

There was a predictable gap in land transactions from 1296 onwards for a few decades but they start again in the 1350s. There were 110 land transactions between 1354 and 1533. Thirty-one mention a boundary with a property belonging to Newminster. As the abbey was drawing an income from its tenancies in the town, the people must have been familiar with the monks and their servants moving about their business.

The abbot of Newminster was involved in the wider political arena of the times. This historian sourced his materials from letters and papers of the reign of Henry VIII:

---

[146] Hodgson, part III, vol I, p 204
[147] Hodgson, Morpeth, pp 46 - 47

The usual conventional pre-occupations are taking less and less of the monks' time. The priors of Durham, Tynemouth, Blanchland, and the abbot of Newminster, are in the main serving the military activities of the border rather than the spiritual.

Situated on the border, a certain amount of responsibility was laid on the corporate institutions which was inevitable. … It was fitting that the abbot of Newminster should ride to meet the queen of Scots at Morpeth in 1515, in the company of lord Ogle, lord Dacre, and other gentlemen. [148]

This anecdote is also recorded by Hodgson. In 1515 a truce was made with Scotland.

"Quhilk time the quene was seik in Morpeth in England, perrell of her lyffe." This was Margaret, sister of Henry VIII, dowager queen of Scotland, who after her flight from Scotland, probably resided in Morpeth castle till lord Dacre, its proprietor, and then warden of the marches, found her an asylum in Harbottle castle. Lord Dacre received her on Aug. 26, this year.[149]

There is a sense of the grandeur of the abbot riding to meet the queen, perhaps on a "caparisoned palfrey", the phrase used by Watkins Williams; a contrast to the first abbot Robert who rode on his "sorry beast of burden".

Changes to the abbey buildings

Although so far I've not found any evidence that the abbey and its buildings were actually damaged during the difficult days of the wars with Scotland, great stone structures on a damp riverside site must have needed constant support and maintenance.

One of the main sources of income for this would be from the sales of wool. We know from Pegalotti that Newminster was still selling respectable numbers of fleeces into the 1300s, but as the years went by, amidst the troubles, it must have been harder to find the necessary money for repairs and new building works.

As for the church, there would during this period be a few changes made to the original simple design of the 1180s which is shown on Victor Ambrus's cover picture of this book. Glyn Coppack, expert on Cistercian architecture who has helped us in an earlier chapter, has studied the abbey site:

There was probably a late medieval re-windowing of the church, especially the gable walls, for which there is a lot of Perpendicular window tracery lying about the site. Stuart Harrison, probably the greatest authority in the country on loose architectural detail, and I have both independently noted a lot of these fragments. [150]

As well as these enhancements, the ARS Ltd report indicates that the abbot's lodging may have been extended in the later medieval period. All this had to be paid for. The donations from benefactors were of great importance.

The lists of benefactors is included in Latin as an appendix to the cartulary (pp 299 – 305), and Hodgson has made a set of English translations.[151] One of the benefactions shows us that costly work was still going on as late as 1429:

Roger Thornton, a burgess of Newcastle, and lord of Witton, who built the castle there, and gave us lead to cover the nave of our church, died on the morrow of the Feast of the

---

[148] Denys Hay, The Dissolution of the Monasteries in the Diocese of Durham, Archaeologia Aeliana, Vol XV, 4th series, 1938, pp 77 – 81

[149] Hodgson, Morpeth, p 167

[150] Coppack, email to author December 2013

[151] Hodgson, History of Morpeth, p 50. Brief notes here helped identify two granges named in the cartulary. Newton grange is Hartburn; Filton grange is near Dere Street in Redesdale.

Circumcision, 1429; for which we say the weekly mass of the Blessed Virgin, and another mass for the dead. They lie in the church of All Saints, in Newcastle.[152]

Such a valuable donation to Newminster must have shown some confidence in the abbey, as well as recognition that serious maintenance was needed.

We can deduce more from the lists.[153] The earliest benefactions show us the familiar names of Ranulph and Juliana de Merlay and Roger and Ada Bertram. As with the charters, the first ones are not dated. From 1336 the dates are recorded, and we can see from this that benefactors continued to support the abbey right into the sixteenth century.

There are two lists and the dates overlap. Those on the first list are from 1336, 1359, 1372, 1377, 1380, 1413, 1416, 1429, 1434, 1436, 1438, 1440, 1468, 1472, 1483, 1487, 1494, 1516, 1525 and 1569[154]. The last two are from the Dacres, the lords of Morpeth at that time:

> Lord Thomas Dacre, formerly lord of Dacre, Graystock and Gilsland, knight of the most noble order of the garter, and warden-general of the marches against Scotland, died Oct. 24, 1525
>
> George Dacre, lord of Dacre and Gilsland, a youth of great promise and the best talent, died suddenly at Thetford in Norfolk, by a fall from a wooden-horse, May 17, 1569. He was under age, and at the time of his death in the custody of Thomas, duke of Norfolk.[155]

Dates on the second list are 1323, 1325, 1346, 1350, 1356, 1361, 1362, 1368, 1372, 1374, 1403, 1480, 1489, 1502 and 1505.

These benefactors are from local families. They include Sir Ralph de Neville, who died in 1368, and who gave the abbey 100 marks at different times. The Lawson family are mentioned as special benefactors; William who died in 1480, Thomas in 1489 and Elizabeth who died in 1505.

The benefactions do not give the impression that life at Newminster was collapsing but rather that the abbey was being supported in its needs.

Changes on the farms

The fourteenth century was a time of change for monasteries everywhere, not just here in Northumberland and the borders. Platt explains:

> Functioning as a demesne farm, directed by lay brethren and worked by a dependent peasantry, the grange in the twelfth century had inspired much imitation by its success. But the expanding markets that had encouraged large-scale agricultural organisation in the early years were to show signs of contraction even in the thirteenth century. By the fourteenth, they had gone into a serious decline. A period of economic depression and political instability, aggravated by extremes of weather, pestilence and famine, set in on a continental scale. Recurring disasters and uncertainties forced on the majority of religious houses an urgent reorganisation of assets. Inevitably the grange was to suffer. The leasing of granges to tenants was familiar already by the turn of the thirteenth and fourteenth centuries. A century later it was general.[156]

Giving examples from the great Cistercian abbeys of Yorkshire, Platt explains that sometimes the lay brothers themselves could become tenants in their own right, or the abbot would let the granges to a single wealthy tenant.

---

[152] Hodgson, History of Morpeth p 51

[153] There are some slight differences between the version in the cartulary's appendix and Hodgson's translation.

[154] This list is from the appendix to the cartulary, pp 302- 304. Hodgson has 1509 for the date of young George falling of his wooden horse, and the cartulary has 1569. The latter seems unlikely, as it post-dates the dissolution of 1537. But Hodgson's dating is out of order, as the previous date is 1525

[155] Hodgson, History of Morpeth pp 50-52

[156] Platt, p 94

To our north, in the borderlands of Scotland, the same process was happening. Richard Oram explains the situation at Melrose:

> By the late fifteenth century, the great complex of property that had been so carefully assembled over the previous 300 years was beginning to be disposed of by the monks. At first, a period of rationalisation may have been in operation, with small, remote or unprofitable pieces of land or rights to resources being sold off or exchanged for ones that lay closer to other more substantial blocks of Melrose interests. The process, however, had begun to accelerate after the disappearance in the course of the fourteenth century of the lay brothers from the Cistercian order generally. In their place, Melrose, like other Cistercian houses, could employ paid servants to work the main granges of the home estate, but elsewhere there was a growing trend towards renting out the property to secular tenants.[157]

It is likely that similar processes took place here. The lay brothers had been fundamental to the early expansion of Newminster's lands. We have seen how the liberty which they exercised in the course of their duties sometimes led to conflicts in the outlying areas on the way to Kidland. David Knowles has this to say:

> The granges, often numerous, were staffed entirely by the *conversi* (lay brothers); a monk was nominally in charge, but it is not clear that he was always in residence, and it must have required more than a little ability to control and maintain in contented employment the large numbers concerned. Often the *conversi* were left to look after themselves, or a single brother was entrusted with a grange as a bailiff. Moreover, the two groups within the monastery had steadily drawn apart: for the choir monks reading and study were taking up more of their time and interest, and agricultural labour less, whilst on the other hand the class of lay brothers no longer contained as its strongest leaven the numerous responsible ex-freeholders and more substantial men who had eagerly joined the ranks of the *conversi* in the early days. When once the strength and simplicity of the spritual purpose had gone, the system was doomed.[158]

This writer does give us one of the few evidences of the number of choir monks at Newminster at that time. He reports that there were 17 in 1379 and 16 in 1381.[159]

Thus, although there is little direct evidence of the changes in how the lands of Newminster were managed and virtually nothing in the cartulary, by comparing with other areas we can guess that a similar process was likely to have happened here.

It was different in the border hills which were in the immediate zone of the hostilities. The great sheep and cattle ranges of Kidland suffered hugely. The abbot no longer sent up the flocks and herds on the great transhumance treks. It didn't pay:

> In times past, when the abbots of the said late suppressed monastery of Newminster thought that the profit taken for the pasture of the said Kidland ... was not sufficient ... (they used to send) ... up their own cattle with their herds and servants in summer time to pasture in the said valleys or hopes of Kidland but their damage and losses were so excessive great as well in the stealing and spoil of their cattle as in the murdering and taking away as prisoners of their herds and servants that always they found the most profit to take ... small agistment in summer time of the townships inhabiting next thereunto ...[160]

This was written after the dissolution and comes from *A Book of the State of the Frontiers and Marches betwixt England and Scotland,* a report by Sir Robert Bowes and Sir Raufe Elleker in 1541. We saw an extract from it earlier, in a vivid description of the *rivelles* and *hopes* of Kidland. By *agistment* the writers mean the hiring of people from the local townships to look after the flocks and herds. Hodgson's full report of this document, which he copied from manuscripts in the British Museum, contains many details about the landscape and lawlessness of this border area at the time.

---

[157] Oram, p 266
[158] David Knowles and Neville Hadcock, Medieval Religious Houses in England and Wales, Vol II, pp 125 - 126
[159] David Knowles, p 112
[160] Hodgson, Part III, vol ii, pp 223 - 224

The devastating war with Scotland, plagues, bad weather, and the depopulation that arose from these all combined to have a negative effect. The old centralised system of farming in the granges by the monks would never return.

Towers against the raiders

One of the consequences of the wars between Scotland and England was the appearance of tower houses throughout the borderland in both countries. There is some evidence that four of of Newminster's properties were fortified in the area of the upper Font and Wansbeck rivers.

The second-last charter in the cartulary is a perambulation of the common pasture of Rothley and it mentions a tower:

> Perambulacio bundarum communae pasturae de Rothlee, capta per dominum Johannem Birtlee, abbatem Novi Monasterii, qui aedificavit turrim de Rothlee in diebus suis …

> The perambulation of the common pasture of Rothlee, held by lord John Birtlee, abbot of Newminster, who built the tower of Rothley in his day … (p262)

This is an undated charter but its location at the end of Gradus VI and the date of the final charter which follows in February 1487 indicates that it is likely to date from the later 1400s.

Two other properties in the upper Font valley, at West Ritton and Nunnykirk, were fortified. Evidence for these is provided in a document from 1547 in the appendix to the Newminster cartulary, in English. The abbey lands were being assigned to Sir Thomas Grey after the dissolution:

> And also all the Grange of Westryghton togeyther with all houses medowes & pastures to the same belongying & a Towre there …

and

> And all that Grange called Nonnykyrke together w^t a Towre there … (p311)

Ritton, from the foundation charter of Ranulph and Juliana de Merlay, later became specifically two granges, East Ritton and West Ritton (p 11). West Ritton tower is what we would now call a bastle, a fortified house. Northumberland Heritage Environment Record 10815 suggests that the thickness of the walls, and the fact that the living quarters were on the first floor, indicates that they are the remains of a defended house

The fourth site is at Greenleighton, a property near West Ritton. In the dissolution assessment of 1536 it is listed as providing revenue from *unius turris cum aliis edificiis*, a tower with other buildings. Northumberland Heritage Environment Record 10787 describes it as having been a bastle with a little barmkin, no trace of which now remains.

These four sites are all in the midway area between Newminster and the outlying Kidland ranges. It may have been worth the trouble and expense of the abbey fortifying these buildings which were in a kind of buffer zone, whereas Kidland was abandoned to its fate.

As for the sisters of Holystone in their priory, they suffered directly from the effects of the troubles. They were repeatedly in danger and at one point had to flee to Newcastle for refuge. Both King Edward II and Bishop Kellawe of Durham gave them financial help and they were awarded benefits from the chapel of Harbottle and the church at Corsenside. In 1375 the bishop of Durham endowed the church of Alwinton to them, and there were various other small grants. But as with Newminster the priory's fortunes were in decline.[161]

Saltworks, cobles and buketts

There is a colourful charter of the late date of 1493 showing that salt workings were still going on in the Cambois and Blyth area. Alex Prestwick was conveying his salt pans to Robert Watson:

> Alexander Prestwyke of Bedlyngton hath selled iiij Salt pannes standynge vp on the north syde of ye Water of blyth w^t all ye app^rtenance yat belong^s, yare to, yat is for to say a cobyll w^t two oyres a rope ij colrok^s ij barowes, two bukett^s and two garners w^t all ye grownde belongynge to yem ..

The abbey's interest in this arrangement is that, upon the death of Robert Watson, it would inherit the cobles (local wooden boats) with their two oars, the rope, the barrows, the buckets, the granaries and all the ground:

> And w^t ye said Alexandr' and Robert ent'chaungeable hath set to our Seales yeuen at Newm' the day and ye yere afore rehersyd. (p195)

The transfer of the property was of sufficient importance that the writing of the charter took place at the abbey, even though the donation would not be implemented until Robert Watson had died.

In the notes at the bottom of the page in the cartulary where this charter is found, Fowler comments: "This, almost the only English document in the book, is printed *ad literam*." And that is what I've done here, with the old-fashioned *y^e* and *w^t* for *the* and *with*.

This is one of the last times we'll need to consult the cartulary in this story. The dissolution of the monasteries is approaching. There are no charters after 1493. I'm closing the book with a little sigh. It has been a very interesting encounter.

---

[161] Dodds, pp 462 - 465

9   Dissolution

Fear and dread
After Henry VIII came to the throne in 1509 who could know that the end was approaching for the abbeys in England and Wales? Newminster had existed for nearly four hundred years. It would surely go on for ever.

But it was the time of the Reformation in Europe and not everyone approved of the monasteries. Cardinal Wolsey, Lord Chancellor of England, discovered that they could be a good source of income and from 1525 onwards he was responsible for suppressing twenty-nine religious houses. Thomas Cromwell was working for Wolsey at the time and he took charge of surveying and valuing them. He then put them up for sale and arranged for the disposal of lease of their lands.[162] He would build on this experience when he later became Henry's chief minister.

In 1531 Henry declared himself head of the church in England, after the Pope had refused to annul his marriage to Katherine so that he could marry Anne Boleyn. By 1533 it became clear that religious institutions which had formerly paid charges and levies to the papacy would be obliged to pay them to the Crown. Henry was looking for all sources of income for his exchequer.

Some of the abbots of the monasteries were beginning to look ahead:

> Far-sighted superiors had read the signs of the times, and had acted accordingly; sheep and stock, the liquid capital that could be realized with the least difficulty, had begun to vanish from the downs and commons, and a process of leasing out lands on a heavy fine for a long term, and of selling or hiding plate and precious stones, had already set in.[163]

At Newminster there is clear evidence that long term leases were being enacted in the second quarter of the 16th century. Between 1527 and 1535 the last abbot of Newminster, Edward Tyrry, enacted some lengthy leases:

> 14 February 1528. Edward, abbot of Newminster and the convent of the same, to Thomas Patynson of Hulkam Grange (Ulgham Grange) the younger. Lease of the grange for life.

> 3 May 1534. Edward, abbot of Newminster and the convent of the same place, to Thomas Abbney. Lease of both the closes called the Horses Closes at the townhead. Term, 60 years. Rent, 16s.[164]

A dozen or so of these leases survived probably because they were still relevant at the time of Newminster's eventual dissolution in 1537 and hence of value to the royal estate.

At the same time patrons of the monasteries, and the descendants of those who had made the original grants, would be wondering if they might benefit from any future disposals and regain ancestral property. They would be discussing their strategy.

What is the abbey worth?
When the end came, it happened quickly. The process was supervised by Cromwell. In November 1534, Henry formalised his break with the Pope by passing the Act of Supremacy. In order to get hold of the wealth of the religious institutions, assessments of their income had to be made. There were three assessments made in quick succession, sometimes partly overlapping.[165]

---

[162] Robert Hutchinson, Thomas Cromwell, Phoenix, 2008, pp 19-20
[163] David Knowles, The Religious Orders in England, Cambridge University Press, 1955, Vol III, p 268
[164] A M Oliver, A List of the Abbots of Newminster, Archaeologia Aeliana, 3rd Series, Vol XII, 1915, p 224. Sourced from Land Revenue Enrolment Books of the Augmentation Office
[165] Wikipedia/Dissolution_of_the_Monasteries and Valor_Ecclesiasticus

Valor Ecclesiasticus – valuation, the first assessment

Cromwell set up an evaluation procedure which became known as the *Valor Ecclesiasticus.* The king also decided to create a new annual income tax of 10% on church property and revenues. Local commissioners for each county were sent out to make assessments between January and May 1535.

The commissioners obtained the information they needed from the sworn testimony of all clergy including heads of monasteries. Newminster was of course assessed. Although many of these detailed records survive, those of some counties including Northumberland are lost.[166] The statistics however were also compiled at the time in a digested form which does include Northumberland and the ever-thorough Hodgson has copied the records for us.[167] At the top of the list for the Morpeth deanery's area is the abbey of Newminster, followed by the churches.

DĒCANAT' DE MORPETH.

Abbathia Novi Monasterij in cōm Northūbland valet in
    spualib₃ et temporalib₃ p anñ c. li. viij. s̃. xj. đ.

        X^a inde x. li. x. đ. ob q̃.

Morpeth rc̃or valet p anñ xxxij. li. xvj. s̃. viij. đ.

        X^a inde iiij. li. v. s̃, viij. đ.

Shipwash rc̃oria valet p anñ lxxvij. s̃.

        X^a inde vij. s̃. viij. đ. ob.

Walton rc̃oria val₃ p anñ xiij. li. viij. đ.

        X^a inde xxvj. s̃. ix. đ. ob q̃.

Ponteland vicaria valet p anñ xiij. li. vj. s̃. viij. đ.

        X^a inde xxvj. s̃. viij. đ.

Heddon Wallen vicaria val₃ clare iiij. li. viij. s̃.

        X^a inde viij. s̃. ix. đ. ob q̃.

Felton vicaria valet p anñ iij. li. xiij. s̃. iiij. đ.

        X^a inde vij. s̃. iiij. đ.

Horsley vicaria valet p anñ vij. li. xiij. s̃. iiij. đ.

        X^a inde xv. s̃. iij. đ.

*Colver vicaria valet p anñ vj. li. xiij. s̃. iiij. đ.

        X^a inde xiij. s̃. iiij. đ.

Newborne vicaria valet p anñ xvj. li.

        X^a inde xxxij. s̃.

The abbey's income from all sources was valued at £100 8s 11d and its tax was calculated as £10 0s 10d. Have a close look at the figures next to *Abbathia Novi Monasterij* above and see if you agree!

Visitation – morals, the second assessment

At the same time as the commissioners were evaluating these properties, another set of commissioners early in 1535 was preparing to be sent out to question the morals, internal affairs and finances of the religious institutions. If it could be shown that these places were not fit to remain open, Henry's case for what was beginning to look like impending closure would be strengthened. These inspections are sometimes referred to as the *visitation.*[168]

---

[166] Knowles, Vol III, p 243
[167] Hodgson, Part III ii, p xliii and History of Morpeth p 47
[168] Knowles, Vol III, p 268

There were four active commissioners sent all around the country to undertake this *visitation*, beginning in summer 1535. Commissioners Richard Layton and Thomas Legh were assigned the north of England, and began their work there in December. By the end of February 1536 they had visited at least 121 religious houses and covered well over a thousand miles over heather, stream and bog, in winter conditions. They visited the abbeys of Yorkshire and went as far north as Bamburgh; they returned south visiting Blanchland, and went on towards Scotch Corner.[169] Not every place was visited and I haven't seen any record of an examination of Newminster. However discussions and fearful predictions would certainly have been taking place within its walls.

At the same time as this was all going on the Dissolution of the Lesser Monasteries Act was going through Parliament and it was passed in March 1536. This gave the king the power to dissolve religious houses with less than £200 annual income as assessed by the *Valor Ecclesiasticus*. As we have seen, this included Newminster.

Comitatus Northumbriae – final accounts, the third assessment

During 1536 the houses with this lesser income were visited again. Yet another set of local commissioners was set up, one for each county. They were to create an inventory of assets and valuables and were able to obtain co-operation from the monastic superiors by promising cash gratuities and pensions. The writing was clearly on the wall – Newminster abbey was among those due for closure.

The commissioners for Northumberland were Lionel Gray, Robert Collingwood, William Green and James Rokeby, the first two Northumbrian and the second two Yorkshiremen. As well as the four commissioners there were three other gentlemen of standing who were to assist with the task. In the case of Newminster they were John Rutherford, John Swinburn and William Green, the last doubling up with his post of commissioner.

The 1536 Dissolution of the Lesser Monasteries Act established that founders or patrons of the monasteries had no right to claims and that all the property would revert to the Crown. Ordinary monks and nuns could either take a sum of money in cash and return to the community or transfer to one of the larger houses of the same order which were still open. A new agency called the Court of Augmentations was established by Cromwell to manage the taking over of the assets and the distribution of pensions. The rights of tenants of the monastic lands were to be preserved.

This time, the full and detailed assessment made for Newminster has survived. It was commissioned on 1 July 1536, and the account was rendered as for the year from 29 September 1536. We can see the first part of this assessment, the *Comitatus Northumbriae,* which is reproduced as an appendix to the cartulary. It evaluates and describes in Latin the abbey's home demesne, then follows with Ulgham, Heighley, Westritton and Nunnykirk granges, Kidland lordship, the saltworks and coal mine at Blyth and the fulling mills near the abbey.[170] After that the appendix only makes brief mention of the remaining holdings.

Hodgson however has abbreviated and summarised the full assessment. This is of the greatest interest to our story as it gives us, in one place and at one date, a complete picture of the lands and properties of Newminster.

The total assets were evaluated as £265 18s 0 ¼ d, a good deal more than the £100 8s 11d of the *Valor Ecclesiasticus.* David Knowles writes:

> On the whole, taken by and large, the *Valor Ecclesiasticus* underestimates the monastic income (or rather the potential income of the monastic estates) by a percentage which is

---

[169] Knowles, Vol III, p 268
[170] Newminster cartulary, appendix III, p 306 – 308

certainly as large as fifteen for the whole country, and which for some districts may be as large as twenty or even forty.[171]

In the case of Newminster the underestimate is huge, £265 being 165% more than £100.

Before we look closely at the list made by Hodgson in more detail, we'll see what other information can be gleaned about the process of the dissolution and the involvement of Newminster.

Faulty monks to be tied up

A natural question to ask is whether or not there was resistance on the part of the monks of Newminster. There certainly was trouble at Hexham priory, only 30 miles away. Like Newminster, Hexham had been evaluated in July 1536 and in September there was armed opposition. The commissioners were prevented from approaching the priory by the canons and local populace encouraged by Sir Thomas Percy, the brother of the Earl of Northumberland. This was part of the general uprising against closure of the monasteries which was taking place in the north and which became known as the Pilgrimage of Grace.

King Henry was furious at this resistance and sent letters to the Duke of Norfolk, who was leading the forces to crush the rebels. Newminster was famously featured in one of these letters.

In 1899, historian Francis Gasquet published his book Henry *VIII and the English Monasteries*. He had studied letters and papers from the time of the dissolution and his writings fortunately for us include a little local information. Here are some extracts from one of Henry's letters:

> Our pleasure is, that before you shall close up our said banner again, you shall in any wise cause such dreadful execution to be done on a good number of the inhabitants of every town, village and hamlet, that have offended in this rebellion, as well by the hanging of them up in trees, as by the quartering of them and the setting of their heads and quarters in every town, great and small, and in all such other places, as they may be a fearful spectacle to all. [172]

Later in the same letter, we learn that Newminster was among those especially named which had offered resistance:

> Forasmuch as all these troubles have ensued by the solicitation and traitorous conspiracies of the monks and canons of these parts; we desire and pray you, at your repair to Sawley, Hexham, Newminster, Lanercost, Saint Agatha's, and all such other places as have made any manner of resistance, or in any wise conspired or kept their houses with any force since the appointment at Doncaster, you shall without pity or circumstance, now that our banner is displayed, cause all the monks and canons that be in any wise faulty to be tied up without further delay or ceremony to the terrible example of others.

The terror imposed by Henry had its effect:

> Under the terror of the royal vengeance, and with the example of these remorseless punishments inflicted on all who came within reach of the royal arm, the commissioners do not appear to have experienced much difficulty in regaining possession of the confiscated monasteries.

> According to the directions given by the king to his generals, the monasteries of Sawley, Hexham, Newminster, Lanercost and St Agatha's were quickly retaken from the monks.[173]

This writer has a most well-referenced account of the closure of Newminster and he includes some information about the valuables at the monastery:

---

[171] Knowles, Vol III, p 245
[172] Francis Aidan Gasquet, Henry VIII and the English Monasteries, London, 1899, p 267
[173] Gasquet, p 268

Newminster was finally suppressed on August 20th (1537) after the commissioners had been there from July 1st. The value of the moveables was counted at close upon a thousand pounds; more than one-half of which was represented by the lead and the worth of 660 ounces of plate. Pensions were promised to the community, consisting of seventeen priests, three junior monks, as well as to four choir boys;[174] but the following year only the abbot, Edward Tirry, and a former abbot, Edward Dunfield, received anything.[175]

The thousand pounds' value of the moveables is astonishing. In modern terms this would be at least £474,000.[176] It shows that Newminster was by no means an impoverished establishment.

Another uncertainty sorted out in this extract is the number of monks at the abbey at this time. Gasquet uses the term *priests* but he presumably meant monks. Thus there were seventeen monks, not the fifteen that is found in many reports about Newminster. It is not a great fault but, with the junior monks and the choir boys, that makes a total of twenty-four, only two of whom received a pension in the end.

The abbot of Newminster and the prior of Hexham were each granted pensions of £30. A reliable source of this information is Denys Hay who also obtained it from the letters and papers of Henry VIII.[177]

Trying to find out what happened to the monks has not been easy. In her article, *The Dissolution in the Border Country,* Susan Keeling writes that the monks of the dissolved abbeys were offered the opportunity to serve in local parishes, including those from the abbeys of Alnwick, Brinkburn and Hexham, but she doesn't mention Newminster.

She surmises that most of the inmates of Northumberland's religious houses seem to have been recruited from local families, and even those who did not continue to serve in parishes or find parochial employment after a number of years, are likely to have remained within the area after the Dissolution.[178]

There has never been much suggestion that the Cistercian monks of Newminster were great scribes or artists, and although they would have had a collection of books, we have no details. Susan Keeling describes the library of the Carmelite Hulne Priory, Alnwick. The house was a poor one, valued at less than £17 in 1539, compared to Newminster's valuation of over £265 in 1536. It at least gives an idea of the sort of books which might have been at Newminster:

> It had a library of a hundred and fourteen books, including, as well as missals, service books, the scriptures and several commentaries, works by St Gregory, St Bernard, St Augustine, Odo, Anselm, Bede and Peter Lombard, histories and chronicles, grammar, logic and philosophy books and twenty-two canon law books.[179]

The quiet disappearance of the cartulary

Newminster's cartulary avoided the upheavals. It must have quietly disappeared in the days before the actual dissolution, when the descendants of the founding family wanted evidence of land grants by their ancestors the de Merlays.

It is in fact possible that the cartulary was compiled from Newminster's charters as one document at this time, or possibly that it was re-copied or rebound from an earlier cartulary. It is significant that the last charter is dated 1493. The charters are not arranged chronologically as they would have been if a continuous record had been kept in a log-book

---

[174] Gasquet, Exch. Aug. Off. Mins. Accts., 27-28 Hen. VIII., 200, m. 4d

[175] Gasquet, as above, 29-30 Hen. VIII., 204, m. Id

[176] www.measuringworth.com , based on RPI 1537 to 2011

[177] Hay, p 110

[178] Susan Keeling, The Dissolution of the Monasteries in the Border Country, in The Last Principality, ed David Marcombe, University of Nottingham 1987, pp 37 and 42

[179] Keeling, p 37

style. They are grouped by families and by geographical areas, although broadly chronological in each section. A quick look back at the pigeonhole diagram in chapter 3 will confirm this.

At the time when the dissolution was pending the lords of Morpeth were the Dacres, so the cartulary may have passed from the abbot to them. The barony of Morpeth passed to the Howards in 1601, after tumultuous disputes between them and the Dacres.[180] We may remember that Rev John Hodgson wrote that the cartulary was with William Howard in 1638. Rev Tanner writing in his 1744 book, *Notitia Monastica*, noted that the cartulary was in the possession of Lord Howard of Naworth.[181] We saw earlier that it was not available to Hodgson when he was writing his history of Morpeth in 1832 but that it turned up again later in the 19th century. We know now that it is in the archives of Castle Howard in North Yorkshire.

There doesn't appear to be any evidence that the cartulary, or any copy of it, was passed with the documents taken from the abbey to London at the dissolution. The thorough nineteenth century historians would surely have found it.

Properties at the dissolution

Now we'll look at the properties of Newminster so conveniently provided by Hodgson.[182] I've put all the places and their valuations on a table, in an English translation.

We can make one deduction with some confidence. The table shows that the monks were no longer directly managing all their lands. We will remember that the system of lay brothers managing the granges in person was coming to an end during the fourteenth century and that the abbeys generally were leasing out land for rental income. The table confirms that this happened at Newminster and it shows many examples of revenue from tenements, ranging from one to fourteen at different places.

Now you and I think of tenements as buildings, often a block of flats, but in this context, the word means *land held by a tenant.*[183] Thus, many of the abbey's former granges were leased by tenants and it looks like they had been broken down into smaller units. Horton Grange had eight; Wreighill, the formerly-named Farnham, had five; and Newton Grange near Hartburn had ten. East Ritton had an unspecified number. Other tenements include five at Mitford, three at Stannington, three at Caistron and four at Eastwick.

Some of the former granges were still listed as such: Ulgham, Heighley, West Ritton and Stritton near Warkworth. There was one that hasn't appeared in the cartulary, at Nunnykirk.

We can see that there were several mills, one at Morwick, two at Stannington, one at Buston, one somewhere else on the Coquet, and two at Newminster itself.

The whole assessment totalled £265 18s 0¼, the valuation precise to the last farthing.[184]

Income from the two rectories at Stannington and Kirkwhelpington with its glebe was substantial: over £7 for the first and over £12 plus £1 for the second, totalling over £20.

The actual home demesne farm of Newminster itself, based at Morpeth and the area around, shows one of the higher incomes, at over £13. But the largest amount of all is income from tenements in Morpeth, at nearly £30. This will probably be from houses on small plots of land, rented from the abbey by the townspeople, examples of which we saw in an earlier

[180] Tweddle, no 4, pp 7 - 8
[181] Rev Thomas Tanner, Notitia Monastica, 1744, chapter xxiv, at the library of the Society of Antiquaries Newcastle upon Tyne
[182] Hodgson, Morpeth, abstracted from p 48
[183] Whitaker's Words, http://archives.nd.edu/words.html
[184] Hodgson, Morpeth, p 47

Newminster's properties in 1536	valuation £ s d
Newminster, the abbey home site or demesne and surrounding lands in Morpeth area	13.12.0
Ulgham, grange	13.6.8
Highley, grange	4.0.0
West Ritton, grange	6.0.0
Nunnykirk, grange	1.0.0
Kidland, nothing but pasture	-
Blyth Snook, seven saltworks, with a granary and coal mine	14.0.0
Newminster, two fulling mills	5.0.0
Morpeth, land and tenements	29.17.2
Chopwell, manor	26.13.4
East Ritton and Healey, land and tenements	10.19.2
Edington, one tenement	4.0.0
Morwick, one fulling mill	3.6.8
Stannington, two mills	4.0.0
Wreighill, five tenements	3.6.8
Rothley next to Riddesdale (Redesdale?), demesne or manor	8.6.8
Stretton, grange or domain	16.0.0
Eastwick, four tenements	2.13.4
Greenleighton, one tower with other buildings	2.13.4
Strother and Hewghe, pasture and tenements	0.13.8
Stannerden, one cottage(?)	0.4.0
Higham Dyke, two tenements	2.13.4
Horton Grange, eight tenements	20.0.0
Newton Grange, fourteen tenements	9.0.0
Tritlington, two tenements	1.9.0
Garresden (Earsdon?) one cottage(?)	0.4.0
Filton and Tolland, demesne or manor	6.13.4
Rothley juxta Cambo, one free pasture	0.6.8
Hudspeth in Redesdale, one tenement	0.6.8
Caldwell, free revenue	0.10.0
Longwitton, one tenement	0.6.8
Warkworth, one saltworks	0.13.4
Shotton, render and revenue	3.6.8
Cowpen, land	0.2.0
Blagden, one tenement	0.2.0
Merefen, one tenement	0.13.4
Choppington, one cottage(?)	0.3.0
Blyth Snook, one tenement	1.4.0
Newbiggin, house or dwelling	2.16.4
Buston, one mill	1.6.8
Horket (Coquet? – Hodgson) Milne, mill	0.13.4
Newton Wood, one tenement	0.8.0
Highley, one close	1.6.8
Saltwick, one meadow	0.2.6
Mitford, five tenements	0.18.2
Stannington, three tenements	2.4.0
Whelpington, glebe of the rectory	1.0.0
Spitall Hill, previously the Hospital of Saint Leonard	1.13.4
Newcastle upon Tyne, eight tenements	4.0.8
Hepple, one tenement	0.13.4
Tosson, tenement called the Hospital of Tosson	1.6.8
Bradeforth, free revenue	1.0.0
Bickfield (Bichfield? Hodgson), one tenement	0.6.8
Chopwell, one meadow called Freremedow	0.0.6
Milburn, one tenement	0.6.8
Flotterton, land	0.2.0
Caistron, three tenements	3.6.8
Stannington, rectory	7.11.4
Bullers Green, xmarum(?)	1.16.8
Whelpington, rectory	12.0.0
Harburn, porc xmarum(?)	3.11.8

chapter. Chopwell in County Durham also provided a large income from the manor there, at over £26.

As for the granges, Horton was a good earner at £20, and Stretton at £16. Ulgham brought in over £13 and Newton £9.

Most of the other properties were providing just a couple of pounds, and in some cases only a few shillings or even pence. Hawk-eyed readers may have noticed that one of the properties had no value at all. Kidland: nothing but pasture. More than a century of border troubles had reduced the green hills to worthlessness.

Under Hodgson's list showing all the lands of Newminster is another one, which is a detailed breakdown of the home site or demesne, the first item in the previous list. It shows all the land and fields in and around the town owned by the abbey, as distinct from the tenements.

Newminster's properties in the home farm at Morpeth in 1536	valuation £ s d
Land in the home farm of Morpeth, with 2 orchards, 3 gardens and 3 small enclosures or closes, containing an estimated 9 acres	0.9.0
One water mill with a small close	3.6.8
One dove cote	0.0.8
One close called *Hungery-hill* with an estimated 12 acres of arable land	0.8.0
Hungery-hill 10 acres of pasture	0.6.8
One close called *Barkerfeld*, with an estimated 16 acres of arable land	0.10.8
One close called *Bromeclose,* with an estimated 4 acres of arable land	0.2.0
One parcel of land called *Burrewod* with an estimated 4 acres of land	0.4.0
One close called *Abbotshaugh* with an estimated 8 acres of meadow, and a parcel of underwood with ash trees and large trees between them	0.10.8
One close called *Bradehaugh* with an estimated 12 acres of arable land	0.8.0
One close called *Cowmedowe* with an estimated 4 acres of arable land	0.5.0
One close called *Northe Parke* with an estimated 4 acres of oak woods with right of pasture	0.4.0
One close called *Southe Parke* of woods with 4 acres with right of pasture	0.6.0
The house tannery, with one small spring (?)	1.0.0
One close called *Wodflatts* with 20 acres of poor meadow with some waste below the meadow	1.6.8
One close called *Oxepasture* with an estimated 16 acres of arable land	0.10.8
One close *Nepp Close* with 13 acres of arable land and one acre of waste	0.8.8
One close called *More Close* with an estimated 10 acres of arable land	0.6.8
One close called *Albaynes* with an estimated 15 acres of arable land	0.10.0
One close called *Newefelde* with an estimated 12 acres or poor pasture	0.8.0
One close called *Esthaugh* with an estimated 7 acres of arable land, of which are 5 acres of arable land and 2 acres of meadow neither one acre ramell (?)	0.12.0
One close called *Greneclose* with an estimated 8 acres of pasture	0.4.0
One close called *Cote Croke* with an estimated 4 acres of arable land	0.6.0
Total	13.12.0

I've put the properties in the main list on a map. We will immediately notice how similar the general pattern is compared to the one in the earlier chapter which summarises those properties from the cartulary over its history. The main difference is what we would expect, the lack of properties near the Scottish border.

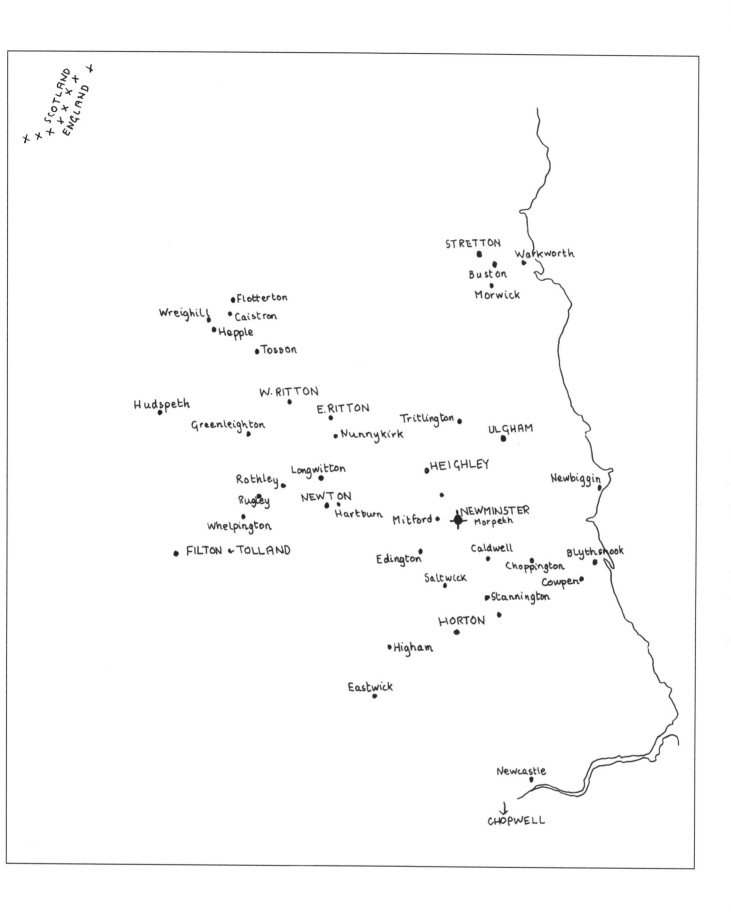

Newminster's properties as listed by the commissioners before dissolution 1536

Morpeth stone robbers

Did local people rob the stones of Newminster? Alec Tweddle commented:

> There is an account that the king's commissioners triumphed, and the abbey was razed to the ground "with the aid of a mob from Morpeth".[185]

How true this is we cannot know. The procedure by which abbeys generally were destroyed must come from other places:

> On February 26 1537, the dissolution (of Hexham) was quietly carried out. Hexham suffered from the vandalism that characterised the proceedings in nearly all the dissolutions of the period. The conventual buildings were destroyed, and lead to the value of £266 13s 4d pulled off them. The church only escaped the common destruction because the inhabitants represented that it was the parish church.[186]

Another account is of the destruction of Roche Abbey, one of the three daughter houses of Newminster, which was dissolved in June 1538. It comes from Michael Sherbrook, writing in the 1560s or 1570s. He was a child in 1538 and when he grew up he questioned his close relatives:

> The Church was the first thing that was put to the spoil; and then the Abbat's Lodginge, Dortor, and Frater, with the Cloister and all the Buildings thereabout, within the Abbey Walls; for nothing was spared but the Ox-houses and swinecoates and such other Houses of Office, that stood without the Walls ...

> The persons that cast the lead into foders, pluck'd up all the Seats in the Choir, wherein the monks sat when they said service; which were like to the seats in Minsters, and burned them, and melted the Lead therewithall; although there was wood plenty within a flight shot of them.

> I demanded of my Father, thirty years after the Suppression, which had bought part of the Timber of the Church, and all the Timber in the steeple, with the Bell Frame ... whether he thought well of the Religious Persons and of the Religion then used? And he told me Yea; For said He, I did see no Cause to the contrary: Well, said I, then how came it to pass you was so ready to distroy and spoil the thing that you thought well of? What should I do, said He; might I not as well as others have some Profit of the Spoil of the abbey? For I did see all would go away; and therefore I did as others did.[187]

A modern description about churches in Coventry and Chester refers to the second phase of the dissolution in 1539. Newminster didn't have bells but otherwise it gives an idea of the systematic way in which the buildings came to be destroyed:

> Cromwell's despoilers were by now well versed in the methodology of dissolution. Once valuable assets like the roof lead had been recycled into 'pigs' or ingots for easy transportation, and the bells scrapped, the stone was sold off as building materials. Recent archaeological excavation has shown that the systematic looting of architectural features and stone was well thought out and disciplined. At the Benedictine churches of Coventry and Chester, salvaged stone was removed in wagons through the great west doors to take advantage of easy access to local highways. A large earth ramp was built up the western steps at Coventry Cathedral's priory so that carts could drive straight into the nave. The wheel ruts in the floors, by now stripped of stone slabs, demonstrate that they then reversed into the north arcade, turned around and came out laden – thereby utilising an early one-way system. The echoing, empty monastic churches must have resembled builders' yards, with material stored in piles, ready to be sorted for sale or re-use.[188]

---

[185] Alec Tweddle, Town Trail no 10, p 29
[186] Allen Hinds, A History of Northumberland, Vol 3, Part 1, 1896, p 160 [187] Platt, 1984, pp 231-232
[188] Hutchinson, pp 201-202

This is a dramatic picture of the destruction of Bordesley Abbey, Worcestershire.

Painting with thanks to architectural historian and artist David Walsh.
© Bordesley Abbey Project

At Newminster, however the destruction happened, and by whichever route the stonework was dispersed, much of it probably ended up in Morpeth. Evidence for this may be seen in mason-marked stones which Morpeth historians have always assumed are from Newminster.

One set of these marked stones is in Old Bakehouse Yard where I live. They are found in an old boundary wall along one of the burgage plots, a medieval dividing wall between the long thin strips of land of the townspeople. Another site where many can be seen is along Bennett's Walk where the lower courses of the stone walls contain half a dozen.

Mason marks on stones possibly from Newminster Abbey

Left, in Old Bakehouse Yard

Next, in Bennett's Walk

Other stone walls and parts of buildings in Morpeth almost certainly contain stones from Newminster. In fact my family house could contain them. Looking around the back alleyways in the town centre is a good way to find them. It is possible that the clock tower may have used some.

The last removal of stone is only just out of living memory. T W Duncan was born in the 1870s. As a young lad in 1880 he helped to lead the last stones from the abbey for building in the town.[189] The Duncans were local bakers, appearing as late as 1958 in local trades directories. T W Duncan may have been from that family. The story appears in one of Alec Tweddle's Morpeth Town Trails. Although he does not say where he found it, the little quote has a feeling of truth about it.

As for the tomb of the Saint Robert, nothing is known about what happened to it.

Mason Marks

The new trainee stone mason was given his personal mason's mark which he would put on every stone he carved for the rest of his life. This mark served two purposes: a mason was paid by the number of stones he produced, and his mark was indisputable evidence of his work; and when the stones were to be fixed in a building, if they didn't match, or were the wrong size, or had been badly carved, then the master-mason knew who to talk to.

Thomas Maude, *Guided by a Stonemason*, p 82

From monks to local gentry
Now my story is nearly at an end. In one of the appendices of the Newminster cartulary is a very long lease, dated 17 December 1547, from the reign of Henry VIII's son Edward VI:

> Assignment by Richard Tyrrell, Esquire, to Sir Thomas Grey, Knight, of the site of Newminster Abbey and its Demesne Lands of Ulgham Grange, etc., for a term of years. (p309)

The name Richard Tyrrell is very similar to that of the last abbot, Edward Tyrry, who made the long leases to local landowners in the decades preceding the dissolution.

---

[189] Tweddle, no 10, p 33

The lease is written in the legal English of the day and the first part of it lists all the closes, or fields, of Morpeth which can be found in the table above from 1536. It goes on to include the land of the granges of Ulgham, Heighley, West Ritton and Nunnykirk and mentions the towers at the latter two. It includes the salt pans at Blyth Snook and the granary there. It also mentions a "Myne of Colles" and a "lytle Boatt or lighter for to carye Colles to the seyd late Monasterye." This seems to imply that coal was taken up the Blyth river as far as it was navigable, so that coal could be transported to Newminster.

The full story of how the lands and properties of Newminster were dispersed is not for this book. There is however a map which gives an idea of what the abbey site looked like after the dissolution, shown on the following page. The map is difficult to date precisely. It is at Northumberland Archives, with a schedule of deeds from the Blackett-Ord estate from 1590 to 1709. There were exchanges of property here at several dates during this period. However, comparing it with another map of the abbey grounds from 1722, this one is clearly in a much older hand and in an older mapping style. It seems surely to be from the 1600s, as it shows quite a few more buildings than the 1722 map. It would benefit from specialist attention.

The one substantial building that seems to have survived by this uncertain date could be the gatehouse, as it is in the right location. It certainly doesn't look like a church. It is possible therefore that the gatehouse was lived in after the dissolution.

It names one field as *Abbey curtayne*. This looks like the central monastic core. The house with the gabled doorway is roughly in the location of the abbot's lodging and so it is possible that this too survived for longer, perhaps as someone's residence.

The map also shows a mill near the gatehouse, and two waulkmills, or fulling mills, as the water channel returns to the Wansbeck. There are a few small buildings and an arched entrance of some kind. These could be the corrodian houses, places where residents paid to stay outside the abbey core. If the map is to be trusted, the church and most of the other monastic buildings, other than a few on the periphery, have disappeared.

After passing through many hands, the abbey site came into the ownership of Sir George Renwick in the early 20th century. We'll meet him in the next chapter.

Following page: a post-dissolution map of the abbey site, date uncertain, but during the 1600s. (At Northumberland Archives, NRO 324-G-01)

Reproduced with kind permission of J H Blackett-Ord

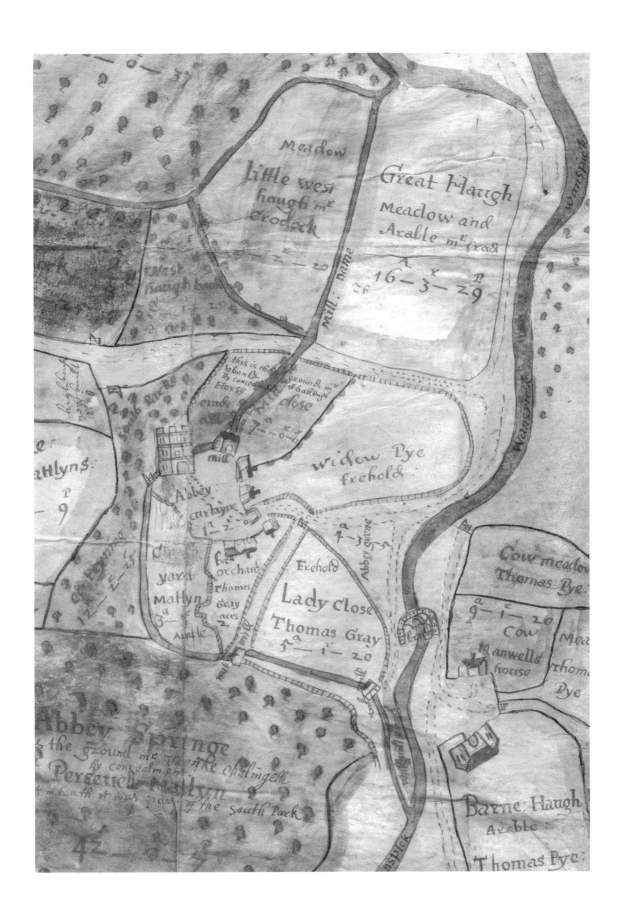

Meadow

little west haugh m^r Crodack

Great Haugh

Meadow and Arable m^r Crad

16 — 3 — 29

West haugh bank

this is the bank by conceal Horse crad

ground m^r Shallong

mill close
7 — 0 — 0

mill. Dame

highland nagfilld

Matlyns
P
9

South Parke

Abbey curtayne
1 — 2 — 0

Widow Pye frehold

Abbey greene

Cow meadow Thomas Pye

clo
2 — 0

orchard
Thomas Gray acres
2

Frehold

Lady close
Thomas Gray
5 — 1 — 20

Manwells house

Cow Mea
9 — 1 — 20
r^homa Pye

yard Matlyn
3

Aintle

Abbey Springe
the ground m^r tonke chalingeth by concealment it in wrath it was of the south park

Perseuel Matlyn

42

Barne Haugh
Arable

Thomas Pye

An engraving from 1816, showing the north window or doorway which was probably reconstructed as a folly

10 Excavations

Early diggers

Newminster Abbey's church, a landmark for nearly 400 years, was pulled down after 1537. Most of the other buildings were destroyed, the stonework disappearing to local uses, much of it in the market town of Morpeth which grew more stable after the union of England and Scotland in 1603. The lands and properties were conveyed into the hands of well-to-do local families. The monastery had disappeared from the landscape but there was always an absence, a sense of something important which was lacking; and some remaining ruined structures, a reminder of what had been lost.

Georgian or Victorian interest in romantic ruins resulted in what may have been the creation of a folly, perhaps by one of the owners. There are a few surviving drawings which show a single arched doorway or window in the north wall, which was almost certainly a reconstruction. Excavations that began in the 19th century are well summarised by Barbara Harbottle in the introduction to her own 20th century works.[190]

The first, which she says "might be more properly termed a treasure hunt", took place in about 1800, when "a stone coffin was found in which were the remains of a young man with auburn hair, which, however, on exposure, soon passed into dust".

Rev John Hodgson, the historian whose work has been such a source of information for our story so far, joined William Woodman, who later became town clerk of Morpeth, in another excavation in 1836. This resulted in little of significance.

Again in 1878, William Woodman directed an excavation, this time with Rev Fowler who we know as the transcriber of the Newminster cartulary and J T Micklethwaite. They appear to have excavated the chapter house and parts of the church but only vague information survives.

Sir George Renwick bought the site of the abbey in 1912 or 1913. From then on, intermittently until 1928, he undertook excavations, and it is the results of his work that are usually seen in old photographs and postcards of the abbey. As well as the church, he investigated the cloister, parts of the east range, the reredorter (toilet block), the infirmary and the abbot's lodging. Sir George was responsible for the re-erection of some of the medieval fabric, in particular the cloister arcades, the chapter house and part of a pier in the south transept.

---

[190] Harbottle, pp 89 - 90

George Renwick and a
member of his staff, at
the north doorway or
window at Newminster,
considered by most
experts to be
reconstructed as a
folly.

Photograph kindly
supplied from the
collection of
T D H Horne

Below, a postcard from
the 1920s after
excavation and
reconstruction by
George Renwick.
It shows the
reconstructed cloister
arcade

It was likely to be George Renwick who collected together various artefacts from the abbey and stored them in a shed near the site, creating a rough and ready museum. The contents of this shed are lost. It probably contained some of the grave slabs drawn by Peter Ryder who had to redraw them from photographs or other drawings.

There was another excavation by H L Honeyman in 1929, about which little is known other than his report on the tiled pavements. The tiles are likely to date from the time of Henry III (1207 – 1272). One of these pavements may have been in the abbey's infirmary chapel, and with the exception of one in Westminster Abbey chapter house, is thought to be the only known untouched 13th century tiled pavement in England.[191]

In situ but badly worn floor tiles. Similar tiles, made from clay and then glazed, would have been used throughout the church, cloister and other monastic buildings. Very few have survived.

From Barbara Harbottle's excavations 1961-63, Trench 17
Interpretation by Barry Mead

Photograph with thanks to the Society of Antiquaries of Newcastle upon Tyne

During the 1900s
Alec Tweddle's Town Trail no 10 gives many details of how the abbey site was used in the first half of the twentieth century by local organisations for their events which include horse shows, garden fetes and a Girl Guides' rally. One outstanding event was a pilgrimage of more than 20,000 people who walked from the centre of Morpeth to the abbey.[192] He also noted an opportunity to bring the site into public hands:

> The Morpeth Borough Council could, indeed, themselves have become the owners in 1965 when 22 acres of Newminster Abbey and other land were put up for sale at the price of £5,000. Morpeth Antiquarian Society requested the Council to purchase it for the Town. This, however,

---

[191] ARS Ltd Report, p 23
[192] Tweddle, Town Trail no 10, pp 29 - 37

it declined to do, stating that it was not so much the buying price that deterred them as the cost of maintaining the abbey and its grounds.

The pilgrimage in 1927

Photograph with thanks to Helen Feeney

Cynthia Fair grew up at the farm which adjoins the abbey site, living there until just before the excavation by Barbara Harbottle in 1961. She now runs a florist shop in Morpeth:

I was born in Newminster farmhouse in 1943. My father Frank Hardy and my mother Isobel had a market garden, a working farm and a dairy there, between the mid 1930s and 1961. My family were tenants. There were different buildings there then, a dairy and a cowshed, pigsties, a stackyard, and a hemmel, and farm cottages. My father grew all the brassicas and salad crops, and some leeks, on the field behind the house and where the junior rugby club field is now.

We used the actual field where the abbey ruins are for grazing, and this kept the vegetation down, and my father would control the weeds.

The abbey site was just a place where I used to play. My parents always warned me to keep away from the wells, and from the moat, because they were dangerous. The water in the moat was quite deep, and there were lots of rushes and yellow irises there. My friends would come down and we would collect tadpoles. People would wander over there and take picnics. Sometimes there was a pilgrimage, and when I was very small these women with funny hats came. I was a bit frightened. I asked my mother and she said they were nuns.

There was a big archway and two rows of arches, probably the cloister, and some graves lying open. Sometimes we'd lie in them and I remember saying to myself: "People must have been small then," because they weren't very big.

The museum was actually just a shed attached to the hemmels, with piles of stones lying about, and broken bits and pieces. There was a box of bones, though, and some mosaic tiles.

My father really minded that the ruins were in such a bad state, with nobody to look after them. My mother used to say that it ought to be made into a commercial venture.

When I think of the abbey, I remember it as a tranquil place, quiet and dignified. Its spirit is still there. It would be a sacrilege to commercialise it with a big C. People used to worship there. That's why it's there. The monks gave work to people. They did good things.

It would always be possible to make a Time Travel type of video, so that people in the future could see what it was like. They could look at it in a museum in Morpeth and then take a quiet walk to feel the ambience of the place.

It should be remembered for good reasons, not just because a king sacked the place. It should be made safe and left like that.

Barbara Harbottle's excavations, the results of which have been such an important part of this story, are the most significant to this day. With the Medieval Group of the Society of Antiquaries of Newcastle upon Tyne, she directed her work in three two-week sessions in August 1961, 1962 and 1963. Many supporting organisations were involved, including Morpeth Antiquarian Society, Durham University Excavation Committee and Morpeth Corporation. Landowners James Steel in 1961, Archibald Armstrong in 1962 and 1963, and tenant F H Hardy all granted permission to excavate.

But, as she wrote, it could not have been done without the "work of an army of volunteers, without whose ungrudging help the excavation could not have taken place".

John Bibby was 13 years old in August 1963 when he helped with the excavation:

In those days, the site was much more open than now and most of Renwick's re-erections hadn't been knocked down, so it was more obviously an abbey. The main area I was digging in was probably the abbot's house. As well as wielding a trowel I was a wheelbarrow man. I would drive the loaded barrows along the planks and tip out the earth and I soon learned not to load them so heavily. More journeys of less weight were more efficient and less likely to lead to disaster. I have a few souvenirs from that time - some oyster or scallop shells, which the archaeologists didn't want. Apparently the monks used to eat shellfish.

Mary Creighton, who lives in Morpeth, was one of the excavators:

I joined the excavation at Newminster part-time, in August 1963. It was a sunny summer, the third summer of the excavations. Barbara Harbottle was a really thorough archaeologist. The work had to be completed in two weeks. I was working on the western part, beyond the church, uncovering stonework. I didn't find anything remarkable, but I do vaguely remember others turning up some human remains. I wonder where they all ended up – there were so many of them.

Barbara Harbottle's was the comprehensive dig at Newminster. The two before that were really amateurish and they made some mistakes with the re-erections. Barbara soon worked out what they'd done. But what really disappointed her was that the excavations had to stop after the three summers. She said there is ten years' worth of work here. Archie Armstrong, who owned the land outside the fence and whose house looked down over the site, wouldn't let her go beyond the fence. She was very upset. It must have grieved her terribly. So she just had to leave it and get on with other work.

Her report is really excellent and covers the work of the three summers. She came along in the autumn of 1963 and gave a presentation to the Morpeth Antiquarian Society. I was always hoping that more work would be done there.

There aren't many people left from Morpeth who helped with the dig. In fact I can't think of anyone. Me – I'm 90 years old next year. Derek Moffat just died last year. He was a real enthusiast at the dig. He was there every day, for each of the three years. He did some of the drawings in the report.

The excavations were reported to the Society of Antiquaries in their publication *Archaeologia Aeliana* in 1964. One of the reasons behind the excavations was the production of the plan of the core monastic site. Most of the monastery's valuables had long disappeared. Floor

145

tiles, yellow, brown and green, were found. Some of them were in mosaic patterns. There were fragments of earthenware roof tiles and brick. A few scraps of clay pipes, some window glass and many small broken pottery items were discovered. There were some iron nails, which would have been used on wooden coffins, and a few oddments of lead including two lead tokens. A find of particular interest was a one-inch long silver-gilt buckle, from the fashion of the period 1270 to 1350, and which is now on display at the Great North Museum. This high-value article comes from someone of wealthy status who had visited the abbey.

Fig. 2. Buckle c. 1" long

A silver gilt belt buckle showing a stylised cloaked dog, dating from between 1270 and 1350, found in almost perfect condition. Approximately life size.

Barbara Harbottle's excavations 1961-63
Photograph with thanks to the Society of Antiquaries of Newcastle upon Tyne

What next?

There have been no excavations since Harbottle's. The next study of significance was the one commissioned by English Heritage, managed by the North East Civic Trust, and undertaken by ARS Ltd, to which reference has been made earlier. It was published in 2011. Here are their summarised conclusions:

- *The site has a huge potential for further research and public outreach but, in the more immediate future, there is a requirement to efficiently manage the structure as it currently stands.*

- *The site has tremendous potential to inform understanding of a Cistercian Abbey, particularly away from the liturgical core where the buildings appear to survive very well.*

- *The earthworks of the inner close, the home grange and those around the periphery of the claustral buildings have a huge potential to inform on the monastic life away from the liturgical core. Exploration of how to exploit this potential could be considered a priority.*

- *There is serious and immediate threat to the Infirmary chapel, where the 13th century tiled floor survives in a currently unknown condition. This, with the exception of the partially modern pavement in Westminster Abbey chapter house, is apparently the only known untouched 13th century tiled pavement in England.*

- *Root penetration is causing, or is considered very likely to be causing, significant damage to the surviving fabric. This vegetation comprises the main threat to the Abbey core in the immediate future and it is considered essential that some form of management must be put in place to prevent any further degradation of the standing remains".[193]*

Four hundred years in existence; four hundred and seventy-seven years of uncertainty. What will happen to the abbey now?

---

[193] ARS Ltd, pp 92 – 97, summarised by Barry Mead

The monastic site lies buried under its mantle of vegetation. Roots may be causing damage to the tiled floor and disturbing the remaining stonework. Ivy is creeping over the arched doorway to the chapter house and the reconstructed cloister. The bones of monks and the donor families are covered up again, under the earth or lying in boxes in storage in the Great North Museum after the excavations. St Robert's tomb has long disappeared.

Local groups would love to see the abbey restored and opened up. It is a place of importance to the Catholic community who revere the first Abbot Robert, their patron saint. There are no rights of way through the site. A thick row of trees screens the view of the site from the paths that go round it. The site is in private ownership and it is the owners who guard it from vandals. Making the stonework safe and preserving what remains is expensive. The abbey is a scheduled ancient monument and the remains are listed as Grade II. English Heritage has placed the site on its Heritage at Risk Register. Its future is uncertain. At the time of writing, English Heritage is working with the owners to understand the significance of the remains of the abbey in their care and develop an urgent repair programme and long-term management plan for the site.

For four hundred years the monks prayed and studied, ate their plain food, looked after the sick in their infirmary and managed their estates. As for the brown-clad monks and the local people who worked for the abbey, who remembers them now? The salt-makers on the snook at Cambois; the carters bringing the salt through Choppington to the abbey; the ploughmen behind the oxen on the rigs at Sleekburn.   Who remembers the shepherds who drove the flocks over the hills from Newminster to the Cheviots, and the people from long-lost villages who milked the sheep and clipped and wove the wool?

There we must leave it. We have been able to explore together some of the secrets of the Newminster story, tucked away in the pages of the cartulary. The essential researches of nineteenth century historians have enlightened us further. Much, much more remains to be understood. Once upon a time, Newminster could be counted among the greatest monasteries in the north of England and the Scottish borders.   For all those centuries, the abbey was at the heart of life in Northumberland. Then its time came to an end. Its fields and granges have long been given over to other uses and the relics of the abbey are lying uneasily in the field, out of our sight.

Seal of St Robert, first abbot, 12th century

Bibliography

Books

Archaeological Research Services Ltd	Archaeological Survey at Newminster Abbey, Morpeth, Northumberland	North of England Civic Trust, 2011
Bailey, Mark	The English Manor	Manchester University Press, 2002
Beckenstall, Stan	Place Names and Field Names of Northumberland	Tempus, 2006
Bede, the Venerable	The Ecclesiastical History of the English People, ed. Judith McClure and Roger Collins	Oxford, 2008
Bond, James	Monastic Landscapes	Tempus, 2004
Burton, Janet	The foundation of the British Cistercian Houses, in Cistercian Art and Architecture in the British Isles	Cambridge University Press, 1986
Caley, Ellis and Bandinell	Monasticon Anglicanum by Dodsworth and Dugdale, Vol 5	1846
Coppack, Glynn	**Fountains Abbey**	**Amberley, 2009**
Craster, H H	**A History of Northumberland, Vol 9**	**1909**
Cunningham, W	The Growth of English Industry and Commerce during the Early and Middle Ages	Cambridge University Press, 1927
Dixon, David Dippie	Upper Coquetdale	1903, facsimile Frank Graham, 1974
Dodds, Madeline Hope	**A History of Northumberland, Volume 15**	**1940**
Fawcett, Richard & Oram, Richard	Melrose Abbey	Tempus, 2004
Fowler, Rev J T	Chartularium Abbatiae de Novo Monasterio	Surtees Society, Vol 66, 1876
Gasquet, Francis Aidan	Henry VIII and the English Monasteries	London, Nimmo, 1899
Gubbins, Bridget	The Curious Yards and Alleyways of Morpeth	Greater Morpeth Development Trust 2011
Hall, Derek	Scottish Monastic Landscapes	Tempus, 2006
Hedley, Percy	**Northumberland Families**	**Society of Antiquaries Newcastle upon Tyne, 1968**
Hinds, Allen	A History of Northumberland, Volume 3, Part 1	1896
Hodgson, Rev John	**A History of Northumberland Part 2, histories by parish Part 3 vol 1, records**	**1827 and 1828 1832**
Hodgson, Rev John	**A History of Morpeth, from Part 2 above**	**1832, facsimile Frank Graham, 1973**
Robert Hutchinson	Thomas Cromwell	Phoenix, 2008
Knowles, David and Hadcock, Neville R	Medieval Religious Houses in England and Wales	Longmans, Green & Co, 1953
Knowles, David	The Religious Orders in England, Vols I, II and III	Cambridge University Press, 1948, 1955 and 1959
Leyser, Henrietta	Medieval Women	Phoenix, 1995
Lloyd, T H	The English Wool Trade in the Middle Ages	Cambridge University Press, 1977
Lomas, Richard	County of Conflict: Northumberland from Conquest to Civil War	Tuckwell Press, 1996
Lomas, Richard	North East England in the Middle Ages	John Donald, 1992
Maude, Thomas	Guided by a Stonemason	Tauris Parke, 2010
Mawer, Allen	The Place Names of Northumberland and Durham	Cambridge University Press, 1920
Newton, Robert	The Northumberland Landscape	Hodder & Stoughton, 1972
Fawcett, Richard and Oram, Richard	Melrose Abbey	Tempus, 2004
Page, William	The Chartulary of Brinkburn Priory	Surtees Society Vol 1, 1892/3
Platt, Colin	The Monastic Grange in Medieval England	Fordham University Press, 1969

Platt, Colin	The Abbeys and Priories of Medieval England	Secker & Warburg, 1984
Plunknett, Theodore	A Concise History of the Common Law	Liberty Fund, 1929, 1956
Prior John	**History of the Church of Hexham**	**Seeley, 1856**
Prior Richard	**Acts of King Stephen and the Battle of the Standard,**	**Seeley, 1856**
Raine, James	The Priory of Hexham	Surtees Society Vol 44, 1864
Roberts, I; Carlton, R; Rushworth A	Drove Roads of Northumberland	The History Press, 2010
Ryder, M L	Sheep and Man	1983
Stevenson, Joseph	**The Church Historians of England, vol 4, part 1**	**Seeley, 1856**
Thornton, G B	The Story of an Abbey and its First Abbot	2002
Tweddle, A H	Town Trails for Morpethians Nos 4, 10 and 29	Davison and Harle, reprinted 2004
Waites, Bryan	Monasteries and Landscape in North East England	Multum in Parvo, 1997
Walbran, J F	**Memorials of Fountains Abbey**	**Surtees Society Vol 42, 1962**
Winchester, Angus	The Harvest of the Hills	Edinburgh University Press, 2000

Journals

Harbottle, Barbara	An Excavation at Memmerkirk	Archaeologia Aeliana 4th Series, Vol 41 61
Harbottle, Barbara and Salway, Peter	**Excavations at Newminster Abbey Northumberland 1961 - 1963**	**Archaeologia Aeliana, 4th Series, Vol 42, 1964**
Hay, Denys	The Dissolution of the Monasteries in the Diocese of Durham	Archaeologia Aeliana, 4th Series, Vol 15, 1938
McNamee C J	William Wallace's Invasion of Northern England in 1297	Northern History Review, 1990
Oliver A M	A List of the Abbots of Newminster	Archaeologia Aeliana, 3rd Series, Vol 12, 1915
Philipson, John	Sites on the Yokeburn	Archaeologia Aeliana 4th Series, Vol 41, 1962
Postles, David	Lamps, lights and layfolk	Journal of Medieval History Vol 25, 2
Raistrick, Arthur	The Great Sheephouse at Malham	J. Bradford Text Soc, 1955
Ryder, Peter	Cross Slab Grave Covers in Newcastle and South East Northumberland	Archaeologia Aeliana, 5th Series, Vol 30, 2002
Scamell, Jean	Robert I and the North of England,	English Historical Review, July 1958
Williams, Watkin	Saint Robert of Newminster	Downside Review, 1939

Glossary

advowson – right to control who should be the rector of the church

cartulary - book containing deeds, charters and other legal records

chaplain – priest of a chapel, under the administration of a parish church choir monks

choir monks – the principal monks at the monastery

demesne farm – the home farm of the monastery

firma – revenue or income

free warren - a royal franchise allowing the holder to hunt small game,

in capite – direct from the king

lay brothers – the layer of monks below the choir monks, who did most of the manual work

messuage – a plot of land containing a dwelling house and outbuildings

obit - memorial service especially on the on anniversary of founder's or benefactor's death

parchment – skin especially of sheep or goat prepared for writing

pittance - an amount of money enabling the monks to have special food on a holy or saint's day

quitclaim – to release from all financial and other obligations

ridge and furrow – rows of cultivated land

rood or rod – a measurement of land usually 5½ yards width by 22 yards in length

stell – a round stone-walled enclosure for sheep

vellum - fine skin of a calf prepared for writing

Appendix 1   Views of Newminster. Compiled and interpreted by Barry Mead

1908 postcard
The archway is probably an 18th century reconstruction which sits on the north wall of the abbey church.

The sign reads: "Newminster Abbey. Visitors are requested to assist in preserving the ruins and not to remove the stones".

The fact that the sign is there shows that the site owner expected visitors or at least tolerated them. A close look at the following postcards of a later date also shows signs on the stonework.

Postcard, probably 1930s or 1940s
This shows the doorway into the chapter house and part of the arcading that ran down the east side of the cloister. These are both reconstructions by Sir George Renwick following his excavations between 1912 and 1928.

A photograph taken in 2011 shows that the reconstructed cloister arcade seen in the postcard above has since collapsed.

This postcard is probably from the 1930s. Neither the arches nor the stone arcade are original; they are later reconstructions.

The western cloister arcade in 2011. This was reconstructed by Sir George Renwick following his excavations between 1912 and 1928.

Appendix 2   Family trees of Northumberland barons

From Percy Hedley, Northumberland Familes
With kind permission of the Society of Antiquaries Newcastle upon Tyne

MERLAY, barons of MORPETH

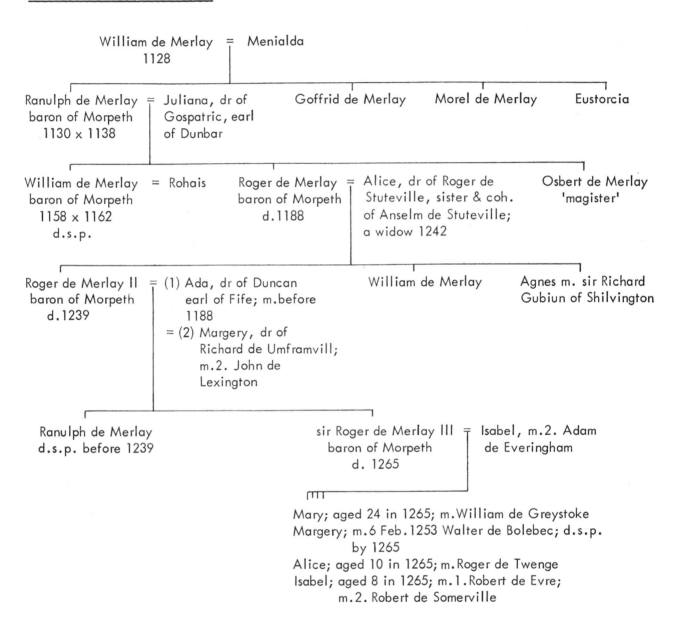

Mary; aged 24 in 1265; m.William de Greystoke
Margery; m.6 Feb.1253 Walter de Bolebec; d.s.p.
     by 1265
Alice; aged 10 in 1265; m.Roger de Twenge
Isabel; aged 8 in 1265; m.1.Robert de Evre;
     m.2. Robert de Somerville

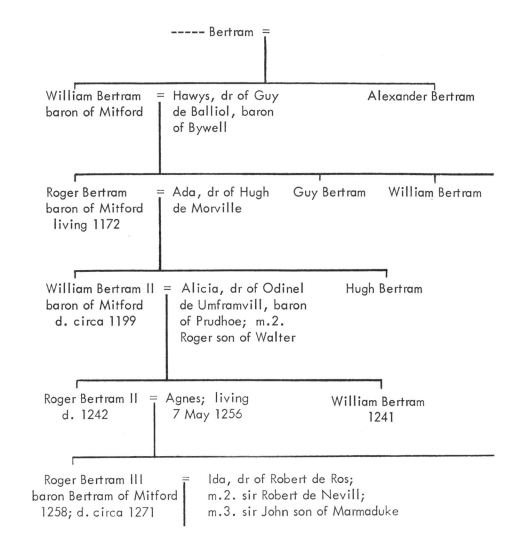

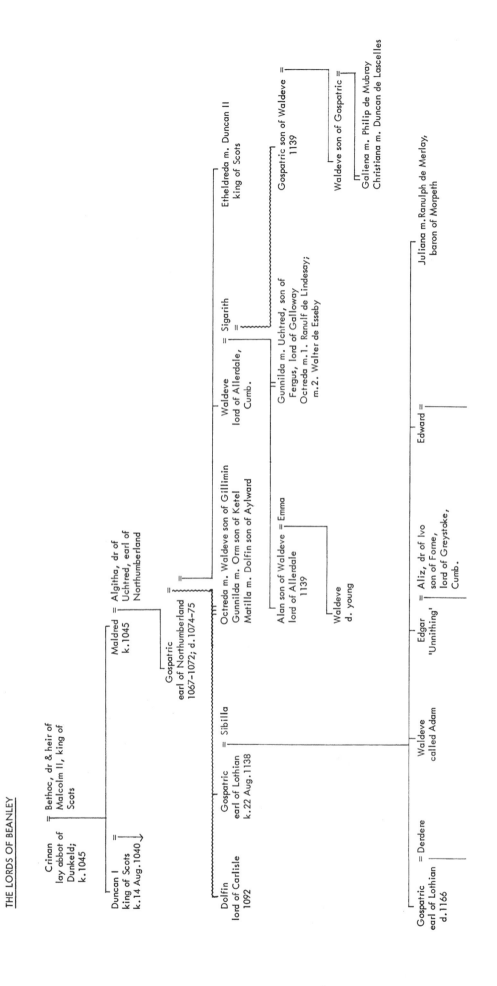

156

UMFRAMVILLE, Barons of Prudhoe

Robert de Umframvill =
baron of Prudhoe
1130 x c.1139;
d. c.1145

Odinel de Umframvill I =
c.1144 x 1156

Gilbert de Umframvill
constable
c.1141 x c.1152

Odinel de Umframvill II = Alice, dr of Richard
d.1181/2   de Lucy

Robert de Umframvill

William de Umframvill
d. before 1195

Gilbert de Umframvill

Robert de Umframvill
baron of Prudhoe
d. circa 1195

sir Richard de Umframvill
baron of Prudhoe; d.1226

Gilbert de Umframvill =

Gilbert de Umframvill = (1) Theophania (widow
baron of Prudhoe, earl   of John son of Hugh)
of Angus; d.1245   = (2) Matilda, dr &
                            heiress of Malcolm,
                            earl of Angus, widow

Robert de Umframvill
of Chollerton; d.
before 1257

= Eva; m.2. Nicholas
  de Bolteby, baron of
  Langley, and 3.
  William de Percy

William de Umframvill
rector of Ovingham

Appendix 3   Latin version of Abbot of Fountains' letter of 1275

Frater Raginaldus, dictus Abbas de Fontibus, dilectis in Christo filiis Novi Monasterii praesentibus et futuris, aeternum in Domino salutem, et finalem in sancto proposito perserveranciam.

Quod ad beatissimi patris vestri Roberti memoriam devocius ac celebrius excolendam, vestra mediante sollicitudine et industria, sex marcharum redditum pia fidelium devocio noscitur contulisse, hoc vestros praecipue ac specialiter animos ad ipsum Sanctum dulcius diligendum propencius honorandum ac fervencius imitandum tamquam filios non degeneres merito provocat et impellit, nos quoque ad Omnipotentis Dei et Beatae Virginis, et ipsius sanctissimi patris honorem et gloriam, mentes vestras et omnium fidelium votis omnibus excitare cupientes, ad peticionem dompni Abbatis vestri et vestrum, consulente eciam in hoc ipsum dompno Geruasio, venerabili abbate de Holmo, tunc praesente, volumnus, concedimus, et statuimus, ut ad dictum redditum sex marcharum colligendum, et secundum quod subscribitur perpetuis temporibus expendendum, aliquis ex vobis providus et discretus specialiter assignetur, qui de proventibus praedicti redditus annuatim circa tumbam Beati Roberti supradicti cereos octo provideat, sicut fieri consuetur. Et insuper, die transsitus ejusdem patris, de residuo quantum se extendere poterit praefati redditus incrementum, conventum vestrum in victualibus splendide procurabit.

Hanc autem ordinacionem vestram secundum quod praescriptum est, tam a vobis quam a successoribus vestris in perpetuum volumus, statuimus, et in virtute obedienciae praecipimus inviolabiliter et immutabiliter observari, auctoritate Dei et ordinis nostri districcius inhibentes ne quis vestrum vel vobis succedencium huic facto aliquatinus audiat contraire, vel dictum redditum ad alios usus praeterquam praenotatum est ullo modo transferre.

Ad hoc eciam, ut haec omnia suprascripta stabiliter in perpetuum perseverent, ego frater R. dictus abbas de Fontibus, dompnus G. dictus abbas de Holme, et dompnus Adam pater vester proprius, in testimonium et muniminem, huic scripto sigilla nostra apposuimus.

Datum apud Novum Monasterium, anno graciae millesimo ducentesimo septuagesimo quarto, die Martis prox. post Ascencionem Domini. Teste Conventu ejusdem domus.
(pp237-238)